Lonely 🌐 planet

THE
LGBTQ+
TRAVEL GUIDE

Interviews, Itineraries, and Inspiration
from Queer Insiders in 50+ Proud Places

ALICIA VALENSKI

Contents

Foreword

All too often, 'word of mouth' is understood in the language of the market, advertising, and communications.

We think of it less as a tool of survival: a whispered historical narrative from the lips of an elder into the ears of their curious descendants; a fiercely guarded tip that opens doors for new community members that have been brought into the fold; a method of vetting, a system of safeguarding, an act of remembering.

For many of us—historians, writers and record-keepers—these spoken exchanges hold as much weight as the written documents we've long been taught to prize above all. We see it as a personal responsibility to capture the fleeting and commit it to the record—records that have often consigned our communities to the footnotes.

Of course, translating the spoken word to the page is never quite the same. Sometimes you lose the gossip, intonations and wonderment that carry the oral traditions that have sustained so many of our overlapping communities. The offhand comments, the spicy anecdotes, the prized folklore are well-known to those of us who are queer, trans, Black, Brown, Indigenous, Muslim, Jewish, disabled, sex workers, refugees and asylum seekers, rough sleepers and countless other maligned identities. From time immemorial, it is how we have kept one another safe.

But arguably, preservation is also a form of safety and safeguarding; a refusal to let anything slip through our fingers. Part of sustaining our collective memory is committing to permanence in whatever form we can. For Alicia and I, that is through the written word.

The work you hold in your hands is another contribution to the global mapping of queer life. Across the pages that follow, you'll hear from queer people detailing their own lives and communities on their own terms.

In each location, what it means to be queer is laid bare. What it means to live in defiance of the margins we're expected to occupy. How we carve out spaces that can hold love, lust, joy, hardship, and heartache. How we claim the contours of our cities for ourselves, spurning the systems that demand our silence and invisibility. How bricks and mortar cannot contain our queerness and, rather, our presence infuses every space, whether we have been established at the center or not.

From bookshops to restaurants and cafes, from local natural sights to strips of clubs, from archives to waterfronts, we seize them all as ours. Spaces where we can commune, connect and extend our network of global queers. Dance floors that have had queer rhythms beaten into them over centuries. Rooms where desire and belonging usurp fear, even if only a momentary reprieve.

This book is but a glimpse of the queer alcoves we have carved out. It is by no means exhaustive, but rather, a mere hint at how numberless queerness is. It is an indicator of how far queer liberation has brought us and how much work still remains, as our queer and trans siblings around the globe continue to live under—fight against and sometimes, die under—homophobic and transphobic colonial legacies on their lands.

Drink in the words committed to these pages as queer people around the globe, experts in their own right, take you by the hand and pull you into their worlds. Together, they issue a promise: we are queer, we've been here and we are simply everywhere.

—Paula Akpan, author and historian

Introduction

I needed a friend.

I was hunched over my phone, nursing an overpriced and mediocre mimosa at the airport in Charlotte, North Carolina, and feeling very alone. I'd spent the last 20 minutes rephrasing Google searches in dozens of ways, trying to learn anything about the queer scene in Playa del Carmen, Mexico, where I was headed. And I had nothing.

I sulkily sipped my breakfast booze, wondering if I should have declined this travel-writing gig. I couldn't find any trace of a gayborhood in Playa del Carmen, so how did I know if it was safe for me to go there as a queer woman? I mean, I knew Mexico wasn't one of the many countries where homosexuality was illegal (or punishable by death—hi and bye, Iran, Nigeria, Saudi Arabia, and Yemen), but that didn't mean there wasn't a stigma around LGBTQ+ culture there. Hell, look at the United States, where same-sex marriage was legal and yet queer people faced discrimination, harassment, and violence all the time. Would it be like that in Mexico, too?

I had no idea. So I, like millions of queer people before me, would have to venture into the unknown on my own, finding out for myself if it was safe to be me. It took a couple of late nights out on Quinta Avenida for me to make a few LGBTQ+ friends who finally spilled the tea on the cool, under-the-radar spots in their city. But it took frustration, anxiety, and feeling othered to find out that Playa del Carmen is one of Mexico's most gay-friendly beaches.

On my flight back to Charlotte, I thought about the new queer friends I'd made during my trip. They seemed so happy to give me the inside scoop, and I was just as happy to receive it. But there was another emotion beyond joy that I couldn't quite put my finger on. I thought about all the times I had gushed about my favorite gay-friendly spots in Charlotte to other queer folks who were visiting or new to the city, and tried to name how it felt. I smiled as I found the word I was looking for—conspiratorial.

I had been given privileged information: an inside look and all-access pass to the way others in the community live in their

corners of the world. Sharing knowledge with this level of authenticity elicits the same thrill as telling a secret—one you only get to know if you're part of the queer kids' club. Whether you're the one offering inspiration or the one looking for it, this kind of conversation is support in action; it gets the word out about LGBTQ+ experiences that are not just safe but also comfortable, enjoyable, and spectacular.

But on the other side of that coin, these exchanges feel conspiratorial because finding out where queer people actually like to hang out in a city is so damn hard. Sure, it's easy to find the tourist traps or the annual Pride parade or the rainbow-washed suggestions from the corporate sponsors. But it's nearly impossible to find out where the community gathers on any ol' day of the year to connect or unwind or let loose; the cool spots they'd bring their own queer friends if they came to visit or recommend to a gay person who had just moved to town. And most importantly, the places where they felt safe to be openly and unapologetically themselves.

Not only that, but I couldn't even find a safe space in a book to indulge my wanderlust and daydreams about trips I might never take and alternative lives I might never live. I couldn't find a place where I could feel connected to the global LGBTQ+ community, to the big picture of what we're all fighting for on so many different frontiers.

I wrote this book to offer an intimate look at the people and places that shape and define the global LGBTQ+ community, creating a safe space where our voices can be heard and our wanderlust satiated.

And it isn't just a travel book with an LGBTQ+ spin on it. It's a proud, panoramic compendium of what it really means to live like a queer person around the world. It centers around people, not just places, with LGBTQ+ locals in each place offering personal portraits, in their own words, of what makes their destination sparkle.

Packed with practical information on what to see and do, and sprinkled with dozens of insider travel tips and inspiration, *The LGBTQ+ Travel Guide* is for readers who don't let their gender expression or sexual orientation hold them back from seeing all the beauty in the world.

In the following pages, queer community members from different backgrounds and walks of life offer honest, helpful insights for LGBTQ+ travelers planning to visit their city, along with inspiration for armchair travelers around the world.

Welcome, dear (queer) readers, to a curated window into the good life, from LGBTQ+ locals who are living well and living whole all over the world.

LGBTQ+ TRAVEL: HOW IT'S DIFFERENT (AND WHY IT MATTERS)

This is the question I've gotten most often as I've been writing this book. As it turns out, I'm not alone in that. Even longtime LGBTQ+ tourism veterans like author and educator **Ed Salvato**—who has been in the industry since 1998, and even leads courses at NYU's Jonathan M Tisch Center of Hospitality about tourism through the lens of queer travelers—continue to get similar comments to this day.

"I hear that a lot: 'Why do you have to segregate yourselves? Everyone's welcome in this place or that place, so why do you have to be different?'" Ed said. "The simple answer is because as LGBTQ+ travelers, we can't assume that 'everyone's welcome' includes us. We just can't, based on our lived experience."

Since 2015, global search interest in topics pertaining to LGBTQ+ travel has skyrocketed. Queer travelers across the world are desperately trying to figure out which countries are safe for us to travel to, and what to do when we get there. And right now, there's not much information to be found—and of that, little of the information actually comes firsthand from other queer travelers.

Likewise, many websites and travel forums don't address the specific concerns of queer travelers, like finding queer-friendly accommodations, bars, or restaurants, or identifying potentially dangerous or discriminatory neighborhoods. Not to mention, sometimes LGBTQ+ travelers are hesitant to disclose their sexual orientation or gender identity on public travel websites or forums in the first place, out of fear of online harassment or discrimination. The internet is basically shrugging its shoulders back at us and saying, "Sorry, you're on your own."

This means that, for millions of people, the thought of a vacation is tinged with a spike of anxiety: they don't know where to turn to find support, strength, and safety to navigate through that anxiety so they can have a relaxing getaway; and they often have to go it alone.

"When people think of things queer people like to do while traveling, they seem to think, 'OK, we'll put the queer travelers we host near where the parties are because that's what they're going to want to do.' But what if you're sober and queer and you want to go do something? If you want to go to the artsy places and not just bars and clubs?"

said **Yasmin Benoit**, an award-winning asexual activist, writer, public speaker, and one of the UK's most prominent Black alternative models. "I think we need to expand the perception of queer travel because most of the marketing you see around it is always focused on Pride and partying, and those aren't every queer person's goals for traveling."

Not only that, but LGBTQ+ tourism overall tends to cater to the young, thin, able-bodied, white, cisgender, male, gay experience.

"We're such a big group of people that have such different experiences with traveling and do tend to need extra provisions. But I find that when companies do tap into the queer travel stuff, it often doesn't get very intersectional," Yasmin said. "When you have multiple intersectionalities, there aren't as many resources you can fully depend on for a well-rounded picture of what a place would be like for you to visit. There might be things for Black travelers, and there might be things for queer travelers, but there probably won't be anything for Black queer travelers. There might be something for men or there might be something for women, but not something for nonbinary people. It gets complicated."

In short, the LGBTQ+ community deserves the same range of travel options as anyone else. Having a diversity of experiences, destinations, and voices is essential for promoting visibility, safety, and acceptance.

HOW TO USE THIS GUIDE

For LBGTQ+ adventurers who may feel isolated or marginalized during their travels, let this book serve as a reminder that you're not alone. Let it act as a reassuring friend, sharing incontrovertible proof that there are welcoming and safe spaces all over the world for you to explore, whether it's from the comfort of home or on the road.

I know firsthand that modern queer adventurers are ready to explore the world beyond just the usual tourist destinations, and we're all seeking authentic, unexpected experiences that cater to our interests and needs. It's time to celebrate the voices that make our community so diverse, as well as to highlight the lesser-known attractions and off-the-beaten-path destinations that are inclusive and welcoming to LGBTQ+ travelers.

And so, I present to you an inclusive collection of authentic profiles covering 20 of the world's most dynamic queer-travel destinations—the places where the LGBTQ+ community thrives outside of just Pride parades. These are places that reflect the diversity in expressions and passions of LGBTQ+ culture, and offer inspiration for the modern queer traveler who is ready for something less stereotypical and more genuine and wide-ranging.

It's my dream for this book to delight curious LGBTQ+ readers and travelers alike by highlighting unique and surprising experiences, and to leave them feeling in awe of the wonderful people and places that exist in the worldwide LGBTQ+ community, regardless of whether they ever get to venture there firsthand.

Most of all, I hope this book will inspire adventurous queer readers to see the world around them—a world that has largely been designed for a heteronormative culture—in a new light.

QUEER-FRIENDLY TRAVEL DESTINATIONS

Cape Town & Johannesburg,

SOUTH AFRICA

RECOMMENDATIONS BY

Yoliswa Moleboheng Mqoco

Between the vibrant vistas of Cape Town and the eclectic energy of Johannesburg exists model and creative consultant **Yoliswa Moleboheng Mqoco** (she/her), whose essence illuminates the very soul of South African style.

"Fashion is a cornerstone of everything I do... and it's not the easiest industry to navigate as a fat woman, a queer woman, and a Black woman," Yoliswa said.

Yoliswa's journey through the fashion world extends well beyond her wardrobe. It's a testament to reclaiming space, amplifying voices, and embracing the beauty of intersectionality.

"A huge part of why I'm still doing this is because the representation I give others means so much," she said. "I didn't have anybody to look at who was like me 10 or 15 years ago. So, I recognize the importance of what I do, and I'm very thankful for that."

Originally from **Pretoria** [near Johannesburg], Yoliswa began visiting Cape Town regularly back in 2015. "I loved the lifestyle here versus back home," she said. "I was inspired by the fashion and how people dress here."

Yoliswa officially moved to Cape Town in 2018. But, as she put it, "Living here versus

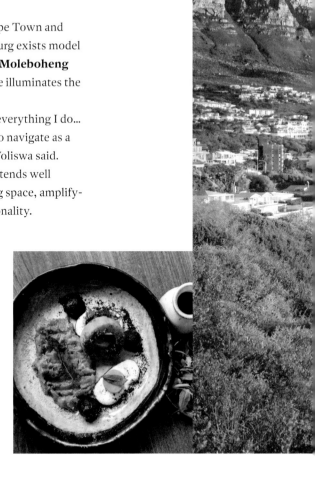

Below: Camps Bay Beach near Cape Town, overlooked by the Twelve Apostles range; Opposite: Eating the rainbow at a Bo-Kaap brunch spot in Cape Town.

KNOW BEFORE YOU GO

LANGUAGES
Afrikaans, English, and Xhosa in Cape Town; Afrikaans, English, isiZulu, Sesotho, and Setswana in Johannesburg

CURRENCY
South African Rand (R, ZAR)

PRIDE CELEBRATIONS
Late February/early March in Cape Town; late October in Johannesburg

WHEN TO GO
South African summer (December–March) for hot and sunny weather, or during shoulder season (March–May or September–November) for moderate temps and fewer crowds

visiting here, they're two different things… It's a beautiful city when you look at it, but it's so flawed when you actually live in it."

In addition to experiencing racism and exclusion from established cliques in Cape Town, the search for other queer people of color to build friendships and relationships with has proven challenging for Yoliswa. So, she has started splitting her time between Cape Town and Johannesburg instead.

"That way I can still see all my friends from back home, have that sense of community, and have a rich life in that way that I don't have in Cape Town," she explained. "It's such a fun city. As a creative—and also being queer—in Johannesburg, it feels different. It feels more freeing. It feels like there's more of me."

Although her time as a Cape Town resident hasn't been perfect, Yoliswa still doesn't dissuade travelers from visiting the city. Far from it. "If you are coming to South Africa as a whole, please do give both cities a chance," she emphasized. "Do not go to one without the other. You won't have a true, authentic experience."

WHERE TO BEGIN

"If you're coming from outside of the country, it definitely makes sense to start in **Johannesburg** because the main international airport is there. Begin there and end in **Cape Town**, which is about a two-hour flight away. Start with the place that has the most welcoming spirit, I would say, then end in Cape Town for a more beautiful experience in terms of aesthetics, food, and relaxing.

"If you're into a more artisanal, curated lifestyle, you'll have a good time in Cape Town. And also if you lead a quite healthy lifestyle, like if you're into hiking and are very active: Cape Town.

"But if you're wanting to really get to know the South African person—especially the South

*Above: Strolling the trails at Cape Town's Kirstenbosch Botanical Garden; **Opposite:** Oceanside dining in Kalk Bay, Cape Town.*

African queer person—and build community, and meet people you could have a possible lifelong bond with: Johannesburg. Johannesburg is much like New York. New York is this melting pot of people from all over the world, and Johannesburg is like that, too. You'll find people from all over the country, sometimes all over the world. And it really is the perfect place to find community, to really have a good time when it comes to socializing and getting to know people."

WHAT TO DO WHERE

"In Johannesburg, there are queer-centered events led by queer people. They create these spaces so that week after week, or month after month, there will be a place where a bunch of queer, Black people will be in one room. I find myself traveling to Johannesburg to go to those events and find more people who look like me.

"My three favorite events are **Pussy Party**, **Same Sex Saturday**, and the **Rainbow Social**—and I'd follow those events' media accounts to keep up with when and where they're hosting things. They're doing so much for our community. Pussy Party also teaches people stuff like how to DJ, and there are many other entities under their umbrella that are useful to queer people. They're an amazing organization of queer-led and women-focused groups.

"In terms of pure relaxation, Cape Town is definitely the place to go. Swim, go to the spa, visit the **Winelands**, go into the city...there are so many beautiful things to do. And you can do them solo or with someone else, and you don't have to spend a lot of money to have a good time. Walking on the **Promenade** and **Sea Point** in Cape Town is free, and it's just such a beautiful experience. Getting ice cream, watching the sunset... **Kirstenbosch National Botanical Garden** is a beautiful thing to do solo, or [go] to the **Norval Foundation** art museum; they're both in the Southern Suburbs...the **Dylan Lewis Sculpture Garden** is, too."

WINING & DINING

"To get the full Cape Town experience, go to the **Bo-Kaap** area, where you can really have an authentic taste experience from a lot of Capetonians in terms of the people that have Malay descendants and the Malay Muslim community.

"I would 100% recommend the **Cellars-Hohenort Hotel**. They put up this huge LGBTQIA+ logo saying that they were queer-friendly, and I almost never see anything like that at hotels. I saw so many people of color that were queer and looked like me. They [the hotel] really are who they say they are in terms of being open to us.

"**Blondie** has delicious Middle Eastern food with a little bit of a Mediterranean influence. It's not actually a queer restaurant, but we often find a lot of queer people there. **One Park** is another good one—it's a bar, gallery, restaurant, and record store. I've found a lot of queer people to be there, too, not that it's meant to be a queer space specifically, but it just naturally happened that way. Next door to that is a restaurant called **Therapy**, which is worth checking out."

The More You Know

"Both cities are beautiful, and each has their own separate issues, so to me, it's important to be as honest as possible when I talk about them. It costs so much to travel, and it's such a privilege to travel. I feel we need to stop romanticizing things and be really honest with people about the cities they want to go to."

Above: *Perfect framing for the* Leopard Fragments *series at the Dylan Lewis Sculpture Garden;* **Opposite:** *Johannesburg's Maboneng Precinct.*

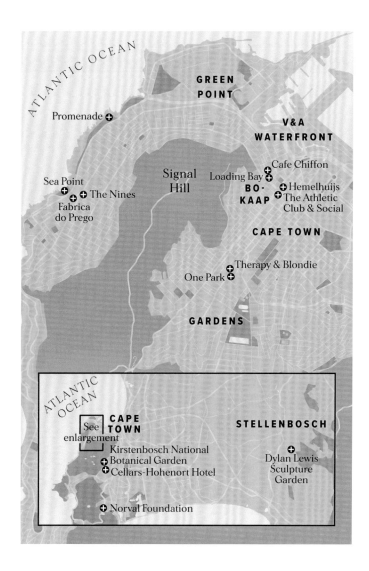

ATLANTIC OCEAN

GREEN POINT

Promenade ✛

V&A WATERFRONT

Cafe Chiffon
Loading Bay ✛
Signal Hill
Sea Point ✛
✛ ✛ The Nines
Fabrica do Prego

BO-KAAP
Hemelhuijs ✛
✛ The Athletic Club & Social

CAPE TOWN

Therapy & Blondie ✛
One Park ✛

GARDENS

ATLANTIC OCEAN

See enlargement
CAPE TOWN

STELLENBOSCH

✛ Kirstenbosch National Botanical Garden
✛ Cellars-Hohenort Hotel

Dylan Lewis ✛ Sculpture Garden

✛ Norval Foundation

More Places to Visit

Hemelhuijs	The Table
The Athletic Club & Social	Ellerman House Hotel
Loading Bay	Seed & Circus
Ken Forrester Vineyards	Cafe Chiffon
Fabrica do Prego	The Nines

Above: Brisk business at a Bangkok produce market.

Bangkok,
THAILAND

RECOMMENDATIONS BY

Pan Pan Narkprasert,
also known as Pangina Heals

KNOW BEFORE YOU GO

LANGUAGE
Thai

CURRENCY
Thai Baht
(฿, THB)

PRIDE CELEBRATIONS
Annually
in June

WHEN TO GO
During
shoulder season
(March–May
or September–
October) for the
best weather

From the main stage of *RuPaul's Drag Race: UK vs The World* to her seat on the judge's panel of *Drag Race Thailand* to her coronation as Lip-Sync Assassin on *RuPaul's Drag Race All Stars* (season eight), renowned Thai queen **Pangina Heals** (she/her when in drag) has long since cemented her place in drag herstory around the globe.

But before stepping into drag for the first time in 2011, things weren't always so glamorous for Bangkok-born **Pan Pan Narkprasert** (he/him when out of drag).

"I was an overweight child. I didn't have a lot of friends. I was heavily bullied. I wasn't confident with who I was at all. I had no real sense of self," Pan Pan recalled. "For me to finally find drag… It healed me. And now it's healing other people."

Pan Pan's drag name, Pangina Heals, is a reference to exactly that—to the way that drag has helped him to heal and has saved his life, inspiring him to love himself in a way he never could have imagined as a child.

FOOD FOR THE SOUL

"Growing up in Thailand, it's like you're blessed but you're also cursed because we have some of the best food in the world—so the relationship you have with food growing up will spoil you for the rest of the world, because wherever you go, the food won't fill your soul like the food in Thailand does. You'll always have a craving for the food back home.

"There's such a huge food culture in Bangkok. It's kind of hard to find food that *isn't* good. Obviously, everyone loves to go into town and just go to all the different street-food vendors. But you have to eat a little at a time because you only have one stomach and there are so many different things to try.

"My biggest advice is: don't just go to what's usually recommended. Go out and find *your* favorite local Thai restaurants. One of my favorites is a little place called **May Kaidee**. It's a vegetarian restaurant, and their pumpkin hummus is truly just the best thing in life. It's always these smaller restaurants where the cooking is what their grandmother and her mother did for generations.

"Seek out where the locals eat. Ask the hotel receptionist, or follow someone who looks like an office worker and see where they eat and what they order.

"The place I usually visit for street food is **Hom Duan**, which is Northern Thai food. They have the papaya salad, the soups, the curries—it just gets it. If you like a Michelin-starred restaurant, I love **Royal Osha**. It's an especially great place to take friends who are not Thai because the food is served so extravagantly, but in a Thai style. The presentation of the food is like a holy experience.

"You *have* to go for a meal along the riverside after dark, because at night you can see all of the temples in Bangkok lit up. My favorite place for this is a not-so-well-known rooftop restaurant called **InLove**. It's by the **Chao Phraya River**, and the food is insanely cheap but delicious, so fresh and local. The ambience is dimly lit and romantic, and there's a perfect view of the **Wat Arun Ratchawararam Ratchawarama-hawihan**, also known as the **Temple of Dawn**, lit up at night.

"Besides that, probably my favorite place to go is the restaurant **Eat Me**. It's a little more upscale, it's dark and sexy, you get to dress up a little bit. It's chic, it's international, like a Thai fusion. The passion-fruit caipiroska is especially good, and it's so refreshing when it's hot outside.

"For a drink during a night out, there are so many amazing cocktail bars. There's one award-winning bar in **Soi Convent** called **Vesper**, where the mixologist is really famous. People in Thailand don't wait in lines, but we did, because the cocktails there are just so good!

"The **Stranger Bar** is a local queer bar that opened in **Silom Soi 4**, which is kind of like a gay street for us—a lot of the places in this area are queer-owned or cater to queer crowds. The Stranger Bar was the first bar I worked at, and a lot of the girls I worked with when I was there are still working there today. The owner is a fellow drag queen.

"There are two 'Sois,' or alleyways, which are considered gay streets: **Silom Soi 2** and **Soi 4**. Those are the most popular places where you can barhop."

Above: Fresh-prepared local veggies at a Bangkok street-food stall; Below: Eating alfresco in the city's buzzing Chinatown.

JOIN THE CLUBS

"The first club I opened is called **House of Heals**. I opened it because there just aren't a lot of drag queens out there who get to perform in a club with good lighting, where the DJs are actually good, and the vibes are curated by a queer person. It's essentially a jungle-inspired drag club, and the girls from *Drag Race Thailand* come here to perform and party and have a good time.

"The second club that I opened is called **Beef**, and it's mainly for bears and bear lovers. And that's another safe space. It's a little bit sexier, a little more on the naughty side. It's all about opening a safe space for people who consider themselves marginalized, whether we're talking about drag queens or bears or anyone else in the queer community.

"Then the third club is called **Rush**, which has more of an after-hours vibe, for anyone who's into exploring their kinky side. There's a subculture of leather and BDSM.

"All three are in Bangkok, all within about 10 minutes of each other."

GETTING OUTSIDE

"One of my favorite things to do is go to **Lumpini Park** because of its monitor lizards. There are literally hundreds of them at a time, walking around like nobody's business. You can take one of the pedal boats out onto the water in the mornings and see all these lizards, and people doing tai chi. It's a nice blend of culture and greenery in the middle of this bustling city.

The More You Know

"At 5pm and 8pm every single day, if you're in a public place and the national anthem comes on, stay still. Because everyone else in the entire city is standing still then. So don't move during that time, to pay respect to the national anthem."

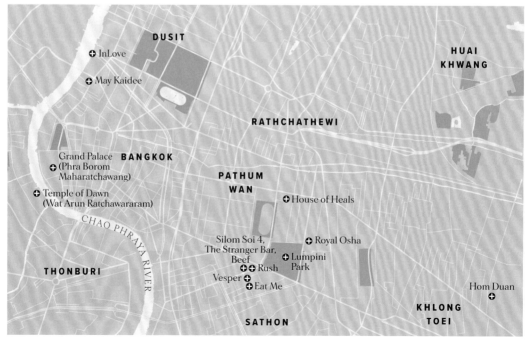

DUSIT

HUAI KHWANG

⊕ InLove

⊕ May Kaidee

RATHCHATHEWI

Grand Palace **BANGKOK**
⊕ (Phra Borom
Maharatchawang)

PATHUM WAN

⊕ Temple of Dawn
(Wat Arun Ratchawararam)

⊕ House of Heals

CHAO PHRAYA RIVER

Silom Soi 4,
The Stranger Bar,
Beef   ⊕ Royal Osha
⊕⊕ Rush   ⊕ Lumpini
Vesper ⊕   Park
        ⊕ Eat Me

THONBURI

Hom Duan
⊕

KHLONG TOEI

SATHON

"As far as getting outdoors, I love **Pattaya Beach** because it's only about an hour's drive from Bangkok. There's a gorgeous beach club I go to called the **Glass House**. You can get fresh seafood there; and **Lan Pho Na Kluea Market** near Pattaya Beach has some of the best seafood in the world. It's a fish market where you can go and pick all the fresh seafood you want and they'll cook it for you right there.

"Another island I love is **Koh Samet**, about two hours' drive from Bangkok, literally known as the 'Gay Island.' All the gays flock there on Fridays and it turns into this crazy party island on the weekends."

THAILAND TRAFFIC

"In Bangkok, I take motorcycle taxis because the traffic in Thailand is so crazy! I mean, I end up having, like, all of Bangkok on my face, because there's so much pollution, but that's fine by me because at least I'm not late.

"It's only a plane ride away to get basically anywhere from Bangkok, or you can take a bus or a train. On the bus, there are usually about eight seats. Always make sure you get the one in the front so you don't get bothered by people; it's easier for you to exit when you get where you're going, and you can get up to go pee if you need to really quickly. If you're in the back, you have to wait, and it's a whole thing. Also, we don't really talk on public transportation."

WEDDING BELLS

"Thailand is the center of one of the biggest moneymakers of tourism in the world and it's gonna be the wedding destination of the world! When they announced that this [marriage equality] bill was going to pass [in March], I got so many bookings to perform at weddings in just one year."

THE LAND OF SMILES

"We're super-friendly people. That's just a part of our DNA.

"In my experience, there are two types of people who come to Thailand: people who come and fall in love with it, and people who come and cannot handle it. Bangkok is a city that elicits very strong reactions. Most people I know come and love it, but some people can't handle the heat, the humidity, the mosquitoes.

"Like with every city, there are many sides to Bangkok. There's the crazy, wild side. There's this serene, sacred side. But I think Bangkok is whatever you want it to be for you. The same goes for the rest of Thailand. It's what you make it."

FIRST-TIMER TIPS

"We have so many temples in Thailand that I love visiting. Obviously, everyone goes to **Phra Borom Maharatchawang**—the **Grand Palace**—because it's one of the most revered, beautiful, culturally important places in Thailand. But you can't wear tank tops, you have to be covered. And

Below: Thai fusion cuisine at the city's upscale Eat Me restaurant;
***Opposite:** Partying the night away at Bangkok's bear-friendly Beef.*

the temples close earlier than you think, too, so I always recommend going early.

"At the Grand Palace especially, I always say that you'll appreciate it more if you read the stories written on the walls, because that's actually the story of *Ramakien* [one of Thailand's national epics]. So, when you read the entire storyline as you go through the space, it feels even more sacred.

"Aside from that, I'd say don't miss out on the chance to get a Thai massage while you're here. In Thailand, an hour-long massage is US$20. And we're known for our massages. A lot of people go to **Health Land**, but there are so many massage places along **Silom Rd** that you can literally just walk into.

"One other thing to know: people are very serious about their heads. No matter how close you are with someone, you don't touch them on their head, because in Thailand we believe there's some Buddha up there. People consider their heads something 'high' on their bodies.

"For when to go, I recommend visiting in April for the **Songkran Water Festival**. It's to celebrate the New Year, and it's one of the biggest festivals we have in Thailand. Because it's the hottest time of year, we celebrate by throwing water at each other. It's really fun."

Opposite: Stock up on fresh fruit— from bananas and coconuts to star-fruit—at floating markets like Damnoen Saduak, south of Bangkok.

Amsterdam,
NETHERLANDS

RECOMMENDATIONS BY

Daan Colijn and Karl Krause

In case the world-famous Red Light District and the litany of coffee shops (ICYMI, coffee shops are for cannabis, while cafes are actually for coffee) didn't tip you off, Amsterdam is a notably liberal city. So, it should come as no surprise that the Netherlands' capital city is something of a safe haven for queer travelers.

For **Daan Colijn** (he/him), a born-and-raised Amsterdammer, this didn't seem particularly notable when he was growing up in the Dutch capital. "I remember, as a teenager, my father would have Amsterdam Pride on the TV because it was broadcast on our local TV network. It was a big deal seeing this representation on TV, and it was so cool that my dad would have it on," Daan said.

But things were different for his husband, **Karl Krause** (he/him). "I'm from a small village in the mountains of eastern Germany, and I came from an area that was not LGBTQ+-friendly at all," Karl said.

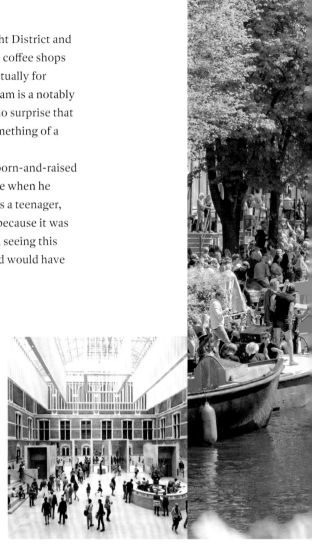

After he came out, Karl moved to Dresden and then Berlin. "My eyes were opened then. It was like, 'This is a community! This is how life could be!' It was unbelievable for me to live in an environment where I had a choice of how I wanted to live, who I wanted to be, and how my life could all of a sudden be."

After meeting in Berlin in 2013, Karl moved a half-year later to Daan's home city, Amsterdam.

*Below: The Canal Parade, a joyous highlight of Amsterdam's Pride celebrations; **Opposite:** Take a culture trip at the city's venerable Rijksmuseum.*

KNOW BEFORE YOU GO

....

LANGUAGE
Dutch

CURRENCY
Euro (€)

PRIDE CELEBRATIONS
Annually from mid-July to early August

WHEN TO GO
April for the annual Tulip Festival, May–June for the best weather, or December for the holiday-season crowds

It was there that they launched their gay travel website **Couple of Men** (coupleofmen.com or @coupleofmen on social media). In the decade since, Daan and Karl have had the opportunity to visit more than 50 countries and five continents together—but to them, there's still no place like home.

"We've learned after traveling to so many places in the world that Amsterdam really is one of the most beautiful places ever," Karl said. "It's so distinct, so different, and has its own vibe that you just don't have anywhere else."

WHERE TO BEGIN

"You can go to **Reguliersdwarsstraat**, the queer street, for the nightlife. **Soho** is a great place to start the night on this street. I used to go there as a teenager when I was growing up in Amsterdam. It's very easy to walk in, very open, with two floors. You can have nice cocktails, it's a very chill place, and it's a good starting point for your night before you figure out where else you might want to go after.

"The other place nearby that our friends always like to go to is **Taboo Bar**, which is a great place to meet people, have a drink, and dance. Another club in that area, which maybe we are starting to feel like we're a little too old for, is **Club NYX**. It is incredibly popular with the young crowd and the ideal spot for newcomers to queer life.

"One of our favorite places is **Spijkerbar**, right near **Leidseplein**. It feels like an old '70s gay bar. You come in and it's dark and you have to walk down some stairs. There's a pool table. They have Naked Tuesdays, which is always a big success. They play porn and animated movies on two TV screens next to each other—if you watch for a couple of minutes, sometimes the cartoon characters will look really happy or bewildered in the direction of the porn, and it's hilarious. It's a

*Above: A marvelous mezze feast in central Amsterdam; **Opposite:** Beers and cocktails at queer-owned Prik.*

good icebreaker if you want to start a conversation with someone. People there are very friendly, and it's pretty cozy."

WINING & DINING

"For cafes that are queer-owned, inclusive, and welcoming for both alcoholic *and* nonalcoholic drinks: **Bar Bario**, **Café Saarein**, **Prik**, **Bar Buka**, **Amstel 54**, and the **Queen's Head**. **Café 't Mandje**—the oldest queer establishment in Amsterdam, originally opened in the 1920s—is a must-visit, too, whether you go in the day or at night. And many more queer bars around the city!

"For good traditional Dutch cuisine and a very old-school atmosphere, we really like **Café Sonneveld**. The cafe celebrates one of our Dutch stars, Wim Sonneveld, a singer, actor, and comedian in the '50s and '60s who was gay but went through most of his life in the closet. A gay-owned restaurant with very Dutch cuisine would be **Pannenkoekenhuis Upstairs**, the smallest *pannenkoekenhuis* (pancake restaurant) in Europe!"

GETTING OUTSIDE

"One of our favorite things to do with friends who are coming over from out of town is to rent a boat. It's just the most beautiful way to see the city. It's about three hours, and you can bring your own snacks and drinks. There are also sightseeing boats of course, but bringing your own food is the advantage of doing it yourself. And you don't need a boat drivers license! You're literally seeing all sides, all the canals and the houses, just floating by. And there are some beautiful lunch places where you could, say, stop your boat and order pizzas, then take them away to eat on the boat and continue your route. We recommend **Mokumboot** for renting your own electric *sloepje* (little sloop boat), but there are also other companies who do the same thing. A good place to pick up pizza from your boat is **De Pizzabakkers Leliegracht**.

"A second place we also like to go is the beach at **Zandvoort**, which is one of the closest beaches to Amsterdam. It's a very popular area for families and people of all ages to go to spend time in the sun. But a lot of people don't know that there is also a nude beach where the gay community like to hang out, between the **Poles 68 and 71**, that's really nice in the summertime. You can use **Restaurant Fosfor** for directions if you have any trouble. Although some cruising does happen, make sure to be respectful towards each other and the other beach visitors who might just be there to enjoy

The More You Know

"Amsterdam is bigger than the **Red Light District** and the **city center**, so make sure you explore the other lovely neighborhoods here. Don't miss out on all the beautiful parks, like **Westerpark**, **Amstelpark**, and the **Vondelpark**... Not to mention the **Amsterdamse Bos!**"

Café Sonneveld ✚

✚ The Queen's Head
✚ Café 't Mandje

✚ Homomonument

RED LIGHT DISTRICT

AMSTERDAM- WEST

Café Saarein
✚

Pannenkoekenhuis
Upstairs
✚

AMSTERDAM

De Trut ✚
✚ Bar Bario
PAMELA ✚

Spijkerbar
✚

Reguliersdwarsstraat
✚
✚ Dragshow Bar Lellebel

ARTIS

AMSTEL

VONDELPARK

✚ Bar Buka

AMSTERDAM OUD-ZUID

✚ Lunchroom Grannies

↓ To Amsterdamse Bos

the sun; and also to respect nature, because the sand dunes here are a protected area.

"Along the same lines, and a little closer to the city, there is the official gay cruising area called the **Nieuwe Meer**. Yes, this is an official cruising area, recognized by the government. Its a nice swath of nature behind the bike path where (mostly) men go to cruise but also sunbathe and hang out with each other. Especially during summer there is a group of men who go almost every day, keeping the area clean but also making it feel more safe. On the other side of the bike path there is a big lake which is great for swimming, and the crowds that go here are a bit more mixed."

QUEER RESOURCES

"If you seek support, community, or further information, then the COC is a great place to start. If you require help because you became a victim of discrimination, violence, or a hate crime, make use of the Pink in Blue specialized police network, who are dedicated to supporting the LGBTQI+ community is these kind of cases. You can reach

*Right: Cycling the city in central Amsterdam; **Opposite:** Party, party, party at Club NYX.*

them by email at rozeinblauw@politie.nl or by phone at +31(0)88-1691234."

QUEER HISTORY

"Definitely go to the **Homomonument**. It's such an important place for our queer community. It's the outdoor space where we celebrate Pride or Kingsday but also come together on May 4 to remember the LGBTQ+ victims of war and hate. What's especially beautiful to us is that although the monument dates back to 1987, it still has so much power, and our community keeps it alive with these kinds of events. The monument is built out of three pink granite triangles, creating one big triangle covering a big piece of the **Westermarkt**, making it part of the city's DNA.

"When at the Homomonument, also check out **Pink Point**, the official LGBTQ+ tourist information point of Amsterdam. Here you can get the queer version of those famous Delft-style figurines of a boy and a girl kissing. But they also have all the up-to-date flyers about events and love to give you information on anything queer."

GETTING AROUND

"The trams, metros, and buses could not be easier. Walk—don't bike in the city center, if you're a tourist—and then when you are exhausted, take the tram. Go out, explore, and try to see more of Amsterdam than just the city center."

More Places to Visit

Westerpark	IHLIA
Club Church	Lunchroom Grannies
De Trut	PAMELA
Dragshow Bar Lellebel	Sauna Nieuwezijds
EYE Filmmuseum	Stedelijk Museum

***Above:** Historic Dean Village, just a five-minute walk from central Edinburgh's Princes St.*

Edinburgh,
SCOTLAND

RECOMMENDATIONS BY

Mairi Oliver

Try as she might, queer bookseller **Mairi Oliver** (she/her) never could keep herself away from her home country for long.

"My family is Scottish, but I grew up abroad," Mairi said. "I came back to attend university in Scotland, then I left, then I came back again...then I left, then I came back again... It just kept calling me back. I last returned to Scotland in 2014 and I haven't left again since, and I moved to Edinburgh to open the bookshop in 2017."

The bookshop in question, lauded as 'Edinburgh's radical bookshop,' is called **Lighthouse**—but it wasn't always. The space used to be home to a different bookshop called Word Power.

"I used to visit it when I was a student at **St Andrews University** up the coast and my sister was at **Edinburgh University**; I'd visit her so I could go to Word Power and find queer books. There was none of that at St Andrews— it was an incredibly straight university when I was there—so I came to Word Power for queer books," Mairi said.

Owner Elaine Henry had been running Word Power since 1994. Once she was ready to retire, Elaine put a call out to the Edinburgh community to try to find someone to take over the shop so it wouldn't close.

KNOW BEFORE YOU GO

....

LANGUAGES
English, Scots, and Scottish Gaelic

CURRENCY
Pound (£, GBP)

PRIDE CELEBRATIONS
Annually at the end of June

WHEN TO GO
During the summer (June–August) for the warmest, driest weather possible

"At the time, I went home and cried, like, 'It's the end of an era!' And my mom was like, 'Why are you crying about this? Go find some money! You could do this,'" Mairi said. "I'd been working in bookshops at that point for the better part of a decade, so I knew how to run one. And so, I bought it. I took a few weeks, renovated the space, painted it, and refreshed it. Made it pretty, made it accessible, clear, and bright, a place you could get around in a wheelchair. It reopened as Lighthouse two weeks after I got the keys."

Considering Edinburgh's storied history as a literary city, it's no wonder that that's where Mairi decided to put down roots when she finally settled back down in Scotland.

"If you're a quiet queer—and I'm a quiet queer by nature, and a bookish queer—then I think it's kind of perfect," Mairi said.

QUEERNESS ALL AROUND

"One of the things I love about Edinburgh is that it doesn't have a dedicated queer area. You get to find your neighborhood and then find community in whatever neighborhood it is. You get to just sprinkle the gay everywhere a bit, and though people will point to **Leith** or to the **Southside**, there isn't just one cool area or a 'gay district' centered around a club area. I think that made it easier for me to live my queerness all around the city.

"Very, very few places feel like somewhere I couldn't go with short hair and a rainbow pin, or my pronoun badges, or whatever. There isn't a sense that places are unfriendly to queer people or an area that feels conservative or that you have to steer clear of—with the caveat that I am privileged to navigate the city as a middle class, cis, white woman."

QUEER LIT

"You can visit the **Lavender Menace** archive. It's full of gay books from the '80s and '90s and it's this lovely intergenerational space. The original founders are usually there—they're in their 70s now—but the people working there range from baby gays that are, like, 18 or 19 to people in their 30s and 40s; it's across the whole age range. It's worth the visit for a bit of history.

"There's also **Typewronger Books**, also queer-owned, and one of the hubs for Edinburgh's zine culture. Tee Hodges, who founded it, is a nonbinary printer who has their own Riso printer.

They run printing workshops and teach people to make zines, and they run an annual **Edinburgh Zine Fair**, which is always worth looking out for. Tee also used to fix typewriters, hence the name. It's a wonderfully weird space, and deeply Instagrammable.

"Down in Leith, you've got **Argonaut Books**, and in **Porty** there's the **Portobello Bookshop**; both may not be queer-run but they're usually full of gays. I mean, the bookshops in Edinburgh...the queers are deeply embedded in the bookshops."

BOOK NOOKS

"Near Lighthouse you've got **August 21**, which is a really cool queer-owned cafe in Southside.

"If it's a nice day, you can sit in the **Meadows**, which is the big park here, and you're close enough to everything at that end of the city.

"There's a really great coffee culture in Edinburgh, so there's no shortage of good cafes. Places like **Fortitude**, **Foodstory**, **Cult**, and **Black Medicine**."

*Above: Continental breakfast, Edinburgh-style; **Below:** Vibrant Victoria St in the city's Old Town.*

WINING & DINING

"The **New Town Fox** is a brunch place near New Town. I have gone there many times and overlapped with a Bears' Brunch, and there's nothing like a bunch of bears in their Sunday-morning fishnet tees having pancake stacks. It's so wholesome.

"You've got **Kafe Kweer**, who do some great vegan food and showcase queer crafts and prints. They're at the **Tollcross** end of town, and there are great walks along the **Union Canal** around that area.

"If you want to drink on a patio, have a good cocktail, and be surrounded by queers, you can do that at at the **Eastway Tap** or **Paradise Palms**. Palms is home to **Saffron Cherry**, an amazing queer POC drag night, and a bunch of other really great queer nights. They do fantastic vegetarian and vegan food, too. You can go for mac and cheese or burgers—it's like vegetarian pub grub.

"The **Regent Bar** is also an amazing gay bar in Edinburgh. It's popular with an older crowd, but it's gay. And one that really does feel *gay*, whereas somewhere like the **Safari Lounge** feels very *queer*. It feels like you're likelier to have more gender fuckery in Paradise Palms or Safari Lounge and meet people across the LGBTQ+ spectrum. But you could still walk into the Regent wearing

The More You Know

"It's Scotland, so dress for rain, no matter how beautiful it is outside."

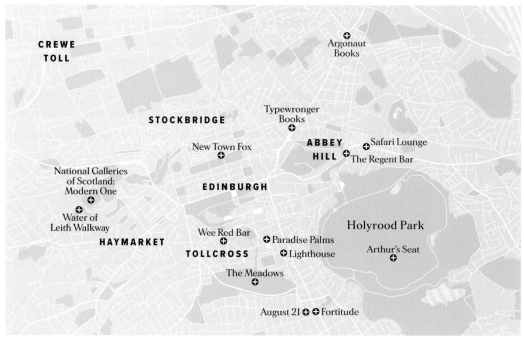

CREWE TOLL

Argonaut Books

STOCKBRIDGE

Typewronger Books

New Town Fox

ABBEY HILL

Safari Lounge

The Regent Bar

National Galleries of Scotland: Modern One

EDINBURGH

Water of Leith Walkway

HAYMARKET

Wee Red Bar

Paradise Palms

Holyrood Park

TOLLCROSS

Lighthouse

Arthur's Seat

The Meadows

August 21

Fortitude

whatever, in whatever setup you are, and feel totally safe and welcome. It's just that it feels more delightfully like an older mens' bar. Queer bars like **CC Blooms**, **Planet**, and the **Street** also offer a big night out, if that's what you're after."

GETTING OUTSIDE

"We're spoilt for parks. Moss dykes are going to have a great time on **Arthur's Seat**. People think of Edinburgh and they imagine the old buildings and stuff, but we have this massive volcanic rock in the middle of the city, and the park around it is so lush. You can really get lost in it, and it's beautiful all year round.

"Then you've got **'Porty' Beach**, as **Portobello** is just 20 minutes from here by bus. One of the reasons I settled in Edinburgh was that I wanted to be near the sea, but in Scotland, 'near the sea' can be hard to find if you're outside of a small village. But Edinburgh has that, just 20 minutes outside the city in Portobello. It's a very visibly queer-friendly space. They have their own Pride in June, and a great queer-friendly bakery called **Go Go Beets**.

Below: Tees and prints on sale at Kafe Kweer; **Opposite:** *Catch live sets, dyke-documentary screenings and rad poetry at the Wee Red Bar.*

"There's the walk along the **Water of Leith Walkway**. You can start at the **National Galleries of Scotland**, which has a cool outdoor space with landscape sculptures. Then you can walk the length of Leith Walk, which has these burbling streams along the way, and lots of birds.

"**Edinburgh Queer Hiking** has hundreds, if not thousands, of members, and they do regular hiking trips. They'll take people who don't live in the city, who are here for a week or a weekend, on guided walks. There's also **Queer Swim Edinburgh**, where they'll take you on a guided tour down towards the **Newhaven** area to places where you can swim. That's especially nice if you're nervous to try wild swimming on your own for the first time, or maybe it's your first time in a swimsuit since transitioning, or whatever the case may be.

"To the same end, the **Edinburgh Queer Facebook page** is also quite easy to join if you're coming for a visit. People post in there all the time being like, 'I'm visiting this weekend, what should I do while I'm here?' And people comment with events that are happening or places to check out. I know Facebook is old-school, but it's a good place to get recommendations."

ARTS-CENTRIC CITY

"You've got **Summerhall**, which is not in itself queer, but it's an art hub. They have a great cafe there called **MF Coffee**, and in what was once the Small Animal Hospital of the Dick Vet School there is now a bar and restaurant called the **Royal Dick**. The indie/alternative art scene also includes **Sett Studios** in Leith, **Edinburgh Printmakers**, **Fruitmarket** and **Agitate Gallery**, who all regularly host queer artists.

"The **Wee Red Bar** does classic dyke-documentary screenings and hosts trans punk bands and rad poetry nights. Very art-school vibes. I'd say several nights a month they host

something queer there. **Queer Film Night** puts on a free monthly screening just over the Meadows in the **Student Co-op**. **Leith Arches** will regularly have something gay going on, too."

GETTING AROUND

"It's a very hilly city. It's a city that's literally built on three layers, where one bit was built over another bit. So, I wouldn't recommend cycling, but it's a great city to walk in. You can walk from one side of Edinburgh to the other in, like, an hour and a half.

"That said, it's not a particularly accessible city. So, if people are mobility-restricted, in many ways, it's not a good city to visit. My sister is a wheelchair user, and if she didn't have a power chair, it would be very hard for her to get around. It's an old city with old buildings that often have stairs only.

"The buses are really good, though. They're tap-on, tap-off with your card or your phone. You don't need to buy a bus pass. The bus drivers are a really good bunch. If you're like, 'Does this bus go here?' they're the kind of people who will actually tell you yes or no. It's relatively inexpensive, too."

Opposite: *Summertime parklife in Edinburgh's Meadows, just south of the city center.*

Lisbon, Cascais & Porto,

PORTUGAL

RECOMMENDATIONS BY

Diana Laskaris and Sue Reddel

When **Diana Laskaris** (she/her) answered a phone call from her wife, **Sue Reddel** (she/her), who was on a Portuguese press trip in 2017, she was not expecting to hear Sue suggest that they should consider moving to Portugal. Sue was a born-and-raised Chicagoan who had never before entertained the idea of leaving Illinois. So what, Diana wondered, could *possibly* have convinced her to relocate from the Windy City to the Iberian Peninsula?

"I said to her, 'You have to come visit,'" Sue remembered. "So, we came back together and spent a week going from the tip to the tail of Portugal, exploring and seeing if I was crazy and I'd had too much wine or if I was correct: that this really was a magical place." As it turned out, Sue was spot-on. Diana fell just as hard for the Portuguese way of life as Sue had.

"I always tell anyone who is coming here to visit: just be prepared, because you're honestly not going to leave," Diana said. "We've been to a lot of places and there are very few places where I've had that kind of special connection or attraction to it. And this is definitely one of those places, not just for us but for a lot of people."

Below: Ornate azulejo *tiles adorn the facade of Igreja do Carmo;* **Opposite:** *Cozy up at the Pensão Amor bar on Rua Cor de Rosa (Pink St), Lisbon.*

KNOW BEFORE YOU GO

....

LANGUAGE
Portuguese

CURRENCY
Euro (€)

PRIDE CELEBRATIONS
Annually at the end of June

WHEN TO GO
Late spring and early fall to avoid summer crowds

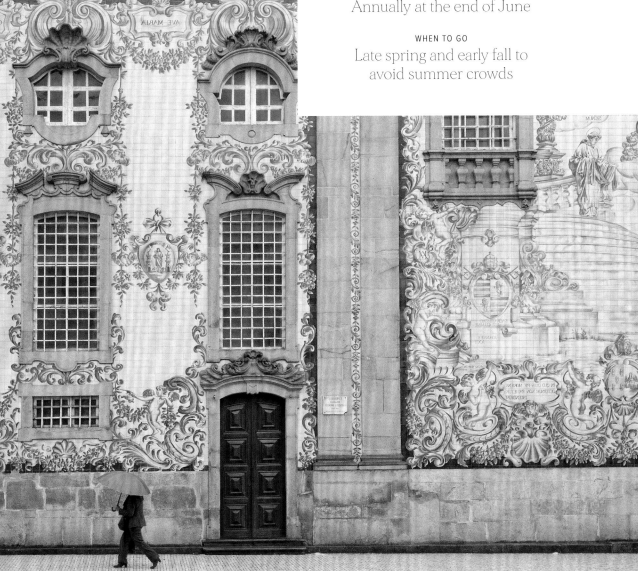

The two travel writers behind the **Food Travelist** packed their bags and moved to a small town in the Portuguese Riviera called **Estoril**, about a 20-minute walk from **Tamariz Beach**, a 40-minute walk to **Cascais**, and a 30-minute drive from Lisbon.

When asked if LGBTQ+ friendliness played into their decision about where to settle down in Portugal, Diana and Sue shared a look that seemed to say "Nah, not so much."

"People ask where the gayborhood is and my first response is: all of Portugal," Diana said. "This is one of the most welcoming places I have ever been. As a foreigner, to feel more welcome than we sometimes felt in our own country, especially as LGBTQ+ foreigners… LGBTQ+ rights are ingrained in the constitution here. No one will bat an eye. No one cares if we're queer. Once in a while someone will ask, 'Oh, are you sisters?' and we'll say 'No, we're married.' And they'll just shrug their shoulders and move on like, 'OK, great,' and that's that."

START HERE

"We would really heartily recommend **Lisbon** and **Porto**. They're beautiful jumping-off points. You can think of Lisbon as kind of like an LA, where Porto is a little bit more like a San Francisco: it's a little smaller, a little quieter. Lisbon's a bit warmer and Porto can be a bit cooler.

"But once you get out of either Porto or Lisbon, there are so many other wonderful things to see and places to visit that are easy to get to. You don't have to rent a car—you can, absolutely, you can drive all over the place here—but you can take the trains and buses, too. The public transportation system here is really great.

"**University of Coimbra** is one of the oldest universities in Europe, and one of the inspirations for the *Harry Potter* films. They have a phenomenal library there and beautiful winding streets.

Above: *Porto's colorful skyline, rising up from the Douro River;* *Opposite:* *Fado players in Lisbon's historic Alfama district.*

Coimbra is also home to fado, a Portuguese style of music that is sort of to Portugal what jazz is to America or what blues is to Chicago.

"Then there's **Nazaré**, which was once a small fishing village but is now known for these massive waves because of the canyon there. If you've seen or heard about the documentary *100 Foot Wave*, this is where it's set. People flock there to watch the surfers try to crest these 100ft waves in the wintertime."

WINING & DINING

"In general, Portuguese cuisine is very healthy. They do lots of grilled vegetables, grilled meats, grilled fish. If you're anywhere near the coastline, you're going to get a fish that was caught that morning.

"**Alto Douro** is one of the wine regions of Portugal. It has these big [vine-covered] terraces that make it a UNESCO World Heritage Site and it's really stunning to see in person. And **Douro Valley** is almost entirely made up of vineyards. There are a lot of places where you can stay and spend a night or two at a wine farm. They usually have really nice restaurants where you can do pairings and all of that. Directly south across the bridge from Porto there's **Vila Nova de Gaia**, which is where all the port-wine houses and port lodges are, and you can do tastings.

"About 45 minutes north of Porto there's **Viana do Castelo**, which is a lovely little place. They have this bakery there called **Manuel Natário**, where a light goes on twice a day and when it does, you'll see a line start to form, because that light means they just put out the fresh, hot doughnuts. They're called *bolas de Berlim*, basically custard-stuffed doughnuts.

"If you go to **Mafra** [part of the Lisbon municipality on Portugal's west coast], where there's the **National Palace**, you'll find Mafra bread. It's well known all over Portugal. It's a specific kind of bread that kind of has a head on it, and it's completely different from the bread where we live. Down here in Cascais, our local pastry is called areias, or the 'sand' cookies. They're somewhere between sugar cookies and butter cookies. All that to say: pretty much everywhere you go in Portugal, you can ask, 'Is there something regional or a local special I should try here?' and they'll usually have something."

LISBON HOT SPOTS

"One of our favorite areas of the city is **Cais do Sodré**, and one of the most popular places for visitors and night owls in that neighborhood is a section of **Rua Nova do Carvalho**, now affectionately known as **Rua Cor de Rosa**, or 'Pink St.' The street is literally painted bright pink, with colorful umbrellas hanging overhead, so it's beautiful to see during the daytime—but people *usually* go there for the vibrant nightlife.

"Probably the most unique place to check out on Pink St is **Pensão Amor**, which used to be a brothel back when Lisbon's Pink St was actually the city's red-light district. The building was restored in 2022 and now offers live entertainment like pole dancing, cabaret burlesque, and more."

JERKS NOT WELCOME

"It's not a place where people need to worry about their safety as an LGBTQ+ person. I don't think most people here care a whole lot. They're more interested in, 'Who are you as a person? Are you a nice person? Are you a jerk?'

The More You Know

"Wear sensible shoes. Especially if it's raining, because those beautiful Portuguese tiles you see are the sidewalk, and it gets very slippery."

Above: *Dressed to impress at Pensão Amor, Lisbon;* **Opposite:** *Custard-filled pastéis de nata, Portugal's signature pastry.*

"Jerks are not welcome anywhere here. One of the first things that we noticed here was the Portuguese will let you go ahead of them. You know, if you're in a grocery store and they see you, you don't have to ask to go ahead of someone with a full basket if you have two items. They just automatically motion for you to go ahead of them. The Portuguese are almost automatically hospitable, automatically welcoming. There's a lot more of a community feel here, a lot more sensibility. It's not as individualistic. The first thought isn't immediately, 'How can I get ahead?' or 'How can I win one over on someone?' It's very collaborative."

FIRST-TIMER TIPS

"Lisbon is built on seven hills. There's a tram that you can take [Tram 28] if you want to see the highlights of all of those hills but don't want to be walking up and down them all day. But it's important to know where you're going, because even if the map says it's half a mile away, that might be half a mile going straight up an incline.

"You can also go a long way on a dime in Ubers and Bolts here, and then a lot of places are even more accessible.

"We think it's important here, and everywhere else, that as a traveler you know where you're going. We've been to places where we didn't discuss that we were married. Those places have a different culture, and we knew that going in. In a place like Portugal, we know they're not very big on public displays of affection in general between adults. You won't see [local] couples of any sort expressing big affectionate displays. So, they wouldn't like that from us, but they wouldn't like that from anyone.

"Overall, out of all the places we've been to—and that's a lot of places—we would, without question, tell people who are queer that Portugal will welcome them. They will have a good time here, there is no doubt about it."

Above: *Queer takeovers are a regular happening at the Tate Modern gallery on London's South Bank.*

London,

ENGLAND

RECOMMENDATIONS BY

Aisha and Lexie Shaibu-Lenoir

Now happily married, wives **Aisha** (she/her) and **Lexie** (she/her) **Shaibu-Lenoir's** initial romantic connection can be traced back to two of London's most notable LGBTQ+ institutions.

The two met for the first time at **UK Black Pride** in 2017. Shortly thereafter, "We bumped into each other at the gayest bar in London, **Freedom Bar**," Lexie laughed. "It's kind of a staple bar for every queer person to go to. I'm sure everyone here has been there at least once to have a porn star martini or something."

Lexie moved to the UK from Paris and has roots in the French-Caribbean island of Guadeloupe, while Aisha was born in London and returned to the city after growing up in Nigeria. "Especially once I was more comfortable with my sexuality, I wanted to be in a place that was open to explore that. And there's no better place than London," Aisha said.

Aisha also noted that London has transformed over the course of her lifetime. "In the past, if you wanted to find anything queer or LGBTQ+-friendly, you'd have to go to Soho because that was the gayborhood. But that's changed and now you can find community across the city," she said.

The Shaibu-Lenoirs have played an integral role in the transformation of London's LGBTQ+ community. In the years since the two first met,

not only have they started their shared LGBTQ+ travel account, the **Queer Nomads**, on social media and joined the leadership team at UK Black Pride, but they have also started their own businesses in support of their queer community locally and around the world.

Lexie founded **Queer Weddings**, providing wedding-planning services for the LGBTQ+ community and adding much-needed diversity and inclusion in the wedding industry. Aisha opened London's first queer intersectional bookshop and events venue, the **Common Press**, in addition to launching **Moonlight**

Experiences, an award-winning experiences and events organization dedicated to connecting queer travelers with LGBTQ+ hosts in cities throughout Europe, Africa, and the US.

"There are so many people in London who have been building organizations that are focused on the LGBTQ+ community," Aisha added. "And now you can see where we are today, which is this beautiful city where you can really find yourself and your people."

TOP STOPS

"There's nothing like **Common Press**, because there are very few daytime spaces for the queer community. During the day, it's a bookshop and coffee-shop vibe. Just outside, there are food vendors during lunchtime, so you can get something to eat and bring it back inside. And in the evenings, there's often something going on. "We love the museums in London. There are a lot of takeovers, for instance at the **Tate Modern**, where they've tried to be more inclusive with their exhibitions than ever before. **Queer Britain**, the UK's first and only dedicated LGBTQ+ museum, is located at **Granary Square** in **King's Cross**.

"Now we have an **LGBTQ+ Community Centre**, too. And **Queercircle**, more of an art exhibition space and somewhere you can explore and learn about queer artists during the day. You can also do things like dance classes, art classes,

language and conversation exchanges, all sorts of cool cultural things there. **Ugly Duck** is another good venue for art exhibitions and taking part in conversations about social issues.

"There's **VFD**, or **Vogue Fabrics Dalston**, a sort of underground venue that has hosted LGBTQIA+ performers and events. **Dalston Superstore** is also a favorite for dancing and drag brunches, and the **Karaoke Hole**—or as they call it, the 'bratty little sister of Dalston Superstore'— is open Thursday through Saturday nights each week.

"And then there's the **Divine**, a new queer bar and LGBTQ+ performance venue that just opened in East London earlier this year."

EVENTS & NIGHTLIFE

"We quite like **Brown Suga** events, centering on Black women and anybody who feels 'othered,' really. Like, those events are somewhere you don't have to come with someone, you can just turn up on your own. And then, all of a sudden, you're meeting friends, because it's not just nightlife focused on dancing or getting with people, it's focused on connection.

"If you're sober or sober-curious there's **Misery**, a mental health collective for queer and trans people of color that hosts monthly alcohol-free events and meetups open to the community.

"For Black and mixed bi, gay, and/or trans men, there's also **BLKOUTUK**, a not-for-profit volunteer collective regularly putting on events

Above: Delicious dishes at Dalston Superstore, famed for its drag brunches; **Opposite:** *Pride on display at the Queer Britain LGBTQ+ museum.*

all over London, from brunches to film screenings to club nights and more.

"There are so many people who have been building organizations really focused on the community. And now you see where we are today, which is this beautiful city where you can really find yourself. And that was not the same 20 years ago, Aisha can vouch for that."

EVERYONE IS WELCOME

"I think you need to treat others how you want to be treated. Because that's what we love and what we want. For us to be able to meet other travelers, traveling ourselves... We also want to keep developing who we are. Personal growth. Travel gives you that. Meeting other people, being able to have new experiences. There's a whole world out there that people don't know of, and they assume that it's something it really isn't.

"When people visit London—even with some of the services I do with Moonlight Experiences for LGBTQ+ travelers, I attract a lot of straight women because they're like, 'I don't feel comfortable going out on my own at night to straight spaces.' Women are seeking safer spaces. Imagine if our society was that safe space and they wouldn't need to seek safety in LGBTQ+ spaces, you know?"

Above: The view from the Tate Modern gallery across the Thames; *Opposite:* Talking the night away at the Common Press, Bethnal Green.

mpstead
ath Swimming
nds

FINSBURY PARK

Vogue Fabrics ⊕ Dalston

The Karaoke Hole & ⊕
Dalston Superstore

La Camionera ⊕

HACKNEY

MDEN
WN

ISLINGTON

⊕ Queer Britain

Jungle Electric ⊕

Colours Hoxton &
Sh! Women's Store ⊕

⊕ The Common Press

Bishopsgate Institute
⊕ LGBTQ+ Archives

LONDON

WHITECHAPEL

SOHO

THAMES

⊕ Tate Modern

SOUTHWARK

STMINSTER

⊕ Ugly Duck

CAMBERWELL ⊕ TOAD Bakery

BRIXTON

"We have a lot of queer nights we can go to, and it depends on what you're after. If you're after a poetry night or a drag show or a party with a good DJ, there's a lot going on in East London."

More Places to Visit

Jungle Electric

La Camionera

Colours Hoxton

Bishopsgate Institute
LGBTQ+ Archives

Sh! Women's Store

TOAD Bakery

Hampstead Heath
Swimming Ponds

The Friendly Society

Two Brewers

Goldie Saloon

Madrid,
SPAIN

RECOMMENDATIONS BY

David Brown and Auston Matta

It's one of those classic love-story plotlines:

Boy meets boy.
Boy marries boy.
They spend a year on an around-the-
world trip, then move abroad and start
a travel business.
Boy divorces boy.
They continue being best friends and
partners in both business and travel.

Well, one of those classic *queer* love-story plotlines, anyway.

Auston Matta (he/him) and **David Brown** (he/him) launched gay travel resource **Two Bad Tourists** after spending 10 years on the road and traveling to more than 60 different countries together, back when they were still married to one another—but they weren't about to let the end of their romantic relationship mean the end of their business.

A quick peek at the former couple's shared Instagram will promptly quash any concerns about bad blood between the now exes. In fact, any strangers scrolling through Two Bad Tourists' recent posts are more likely to assume that the two are still together.

"Just like any LGBTQ+ person is never really finished coming out—they'll continue to come

Below: Be sure to check out picture-perfect Madrid squares like storied Plaza Mayor; *Opposite:* City-center Café Comercial, serving Madrid in style since 1897.

KNOW BEFORE YOU GO

· ·

LANGUAGE
Spanish

CURRENCY
Euro (€)

PRIDE CELEBRATIONS
Annually during the first
weekend in July

WHEN TO GO
During shoulder season (March–June
or September–November) for the
best weather: sunny and temperate,
but not excessively hot or cold

out again and again for the rest of their lives—we will have to continue to come out as broken up for the rest of our lives," Auston laughed.

Still best friends and business partners, David and Auston continue to live (separately) in Madrid, where they organize local LGBTQ+ tapas and nightlife tours for gay travelers visiting the Spanish capital from all around the world.

When the two moved to Madrid in 2013, they were originally looking for a big-city atmosphere and a chance to learn how to speak Spanish. But they came across something that did an even better job of convincing them that Madrid was the right move for their lifestyle.

"When we were in Madrid, we saw gay couples—of course in **Chueca**, but also all around the center outside of that specifically queer neighborhood—holding hands and being affectionate," David said. "It really felt like the whole city was a safe space."

"Particularly when you walk through the center, it's just so queer," Auston said.

"It's absurdly queer," David said.

"It's absurdly queer," Auston confirmed.

WHERE TO BEGIN

"**Plaza de Chueca** is the number-one spot to go first; it's kind of like the place to 'see and be seen.' There are a bunch of terraces, so you can sit down and people-watch to get an idea of what the vibe is like. The metro there is also rainbow-colored to embrace the queer identity of Chueca, so you know you're in the heart of it.

"When you walk around Chueca, there are so many different gay bars and bookshops and restaurants that are queer-friendly. You can just walk around and have an overall queer experience. I think there are something like 200 LGBTQ+ venues—whether it's a gay club, sauna, cafe—and you can just wander around for hours and sort of be immersed in the queer neighborhood."

Above: *The city's Puerta de Alcalá, rainbow-lit for WorldPride Week;* **Opposite:** *Chili-laced mussels on the tapas menu in Madrid.*

WINING

"**La Kama Café** is a really good one for sitting down and having cocktails. Spain doesn't really do 'cocktail culture'—it's a lot of beer, wine, or mixed drinks like gin and tonics or rum and cokes. So, for a lot of foreigners, it's nice to start at a place where you can get a proper cocktail. La Kama Café is a good one for that because you can get your cosmos [cosmopolitans], your margaritas, all of those cocktails you can't really get when you go to a typical bar in Spain... and it doesn't hurt that their servers are super *guapo* [handsome].

"I think it's always great to start out by giving people what they want (in this case, the cocktails that they're used to) to make them comfortable. But then we also want to push their limits a little, so they get more into the Spanish culture. That's when we'd move on to *vermut* [vermouth], a very typical *aperitivo* you'd have before your dinner. **Casa Camacho** is a good place for that... They're a *vermuteria*, so they produce their own vermouth there in the neighborhood of Chueca. So that's a good spot to introduce people to something they may not usually order."

DINING

"Kitchens don't open for dinner until about 8pm, sometimes 8:30pm. So don't expect to be able to eat dinner at 6pm or 7pm. You'll have to find a kitchen that's 'all-day' if you want that. Some do exist, but at the best restaurants you're going to be eating around 9pm or 10pm, for sure.

"You can try some typical tapas while you're at Casa Camacho. There's one called *gilda* from the north of Spain that has a pepper, an olive, and an anchovy on a skewer, which is nice. And the *ensaladilla rusa*, the Russian salad, is a very typical tapa as well. So now they're trying new things, pushing their limits a little bit.

"A *bocadillo de calamares*, a calamari sandwich, is a really popular thing to eat here, too. There's a place called **La Campana** that's known for it. Highly recommend.

"There's a market we like to go to called **Mercado San Antón**. It has a bunch of different stalls, so you can try different tapas and things. And it's very visual, so if you don't know Spanish food, it's a great way to get started. Like, 'That looks good, I'll order that.'

"They've got a wine bar, they have an outdoor terrace, they have great gin and tonics, and they have a restaurant if you want to sit down and eat. And it's right in Chueca, so that's a really good spot for food and drinks.

The More You Know

"Don't expect that everyone is going to speak English. It's funny because you'll go to some places and people will have a great level of English, then you'll go to the next place and they won't speak a word of English, and you have to be able to get by."

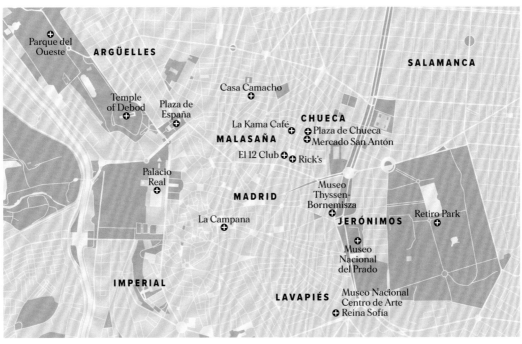

"You could order churros, but there's also another version called *porras*, which are kind of a thicker version—eat some of those with chocolate. And don't order sangria, order *tinto de verano* [Spanish red-wine cocktail]. It's just a more common drink."

PARTY CITY

"Madrid is a party city. Spanish people in general want to be on the street having a party. They don't always even care what it is. They're like, 'Let's do the *botellón*: drink on the street, listen to live music...' But Madrid in particular—compared to any other place, even more so than Barcelona and other cities in Spain—any time there's a big holiday weekend or New Year's, they just throw parties. You'll always find gay-specific parties around them.

"Clubs open at midnight and don't get going until like, 2am, so don't go any time before (or even right at) midnight. But around 1am to 2am is the time to trickle in. Be ready to be out until 6am, for sure.

Below: Fabulous blooms for sale at Madrid's Atocha train station; Opposite: Paddle power at Retiro Park in central Madrid.

"Later in the night, we would go to... Well, it also changes with your generation, right? Because 10 years ago, we were not 40 years old, so our 'place to go' is different now.

"So now, 'the place' is called **El 12 Club**. It's kind of like, 30s, 40s, and 50s, that's where all the gays are going now. That's where we end up at night. That's where you're going to get your beer or your gin and tonics. No more margaritas, no more cosmos—you have to go to special places for those.

"When we were younger, we would go to **DLRO**. It probably trends more 20s to 30s. But it was one of the places where it didn't matter what night of the week it was, you could go and it would be open, and there would be people dancing until like 6am. Like, every night. And I think they still have that sort of 'claim to fame.'

"We would go to **Rick's** now. It skews like 40s to 50s and 60s, but I like that, because it's a very different vibe from going out with people who are in their 20s."

TO-DO LIST

"We're obviously biased because we offer one, but: go on a food tour! Find the best restaurants to go to and do your own self-guided tapas tour, or find a company and book one. It's such a cool and authentic way to get to know the city, because Madrid food is going to be different to Sevilla food, which is different from Valencia... So, you can get not just a taste of Spain but a very Madrid kind of experience. And who doesn't love eating, and drinking wine or beer?

"If you're into outdoors stuff, you should go to **Retiro Park**. It's kind of the main city park, and it's quite beautiful, so a lot of people go there.

"For cultural sights, the **Palacio Real** is great. You could just see it from the outside, but you can also do a tour inside. And, of course, visit all the main squares: **Plaza de España**, **Puerta del Sol**,

Plaza Mayor. There's also an Egyptian temple called **Temple of Debod** in a nice park area, **Parque del Oeste**, so that's an interesting thing about the city.

"If you're an art buff, Madrid is also known for what's called the 'Golden Triangle' of art: **Museo Nacional del Prado**, **Museo Nacional Centro de Arte Reina Sofía**, and **Museo Thyssen-Bornemisza**.

"Even if you're not an art buff, we actually visited this special queer exhibit at the Thyssen called **Inclusive Love**. It's an audio guide that takes you around the artwork throughout the museum that has queer history or another LGBTQ+ element to it—either the artists themselves were queer, the subject of the work is a part of the LGBTQ+ community, or something else about the piece is queer-oriented. We're not even super into art but it was cool to see how they connected all of these works with this underlying theme of inclusivity."

Opposite: Take a wander among old masters at Madrid's world-renowned Museo Nacional del Prado, in the city's 'Golden Triangle' of art.

Above: *Street art in Milan's boho Ticinese district.*

Milan,
ITALY

RECOMMENDATIONS BY

Daniele Catena and Luigi Cocciolo

KNOW BEFORE YOU GO

LANGUAGE
Italian

CURRENCY
Euro (€)

PRIDE CELEBRATIONS
Annually at the end of June

WHEN TO GO
During shoulder season (April–June and September–October) for mild weather and fewer crowds

Long before **Daniele Catena** (he/him) and **Luigi Cocciolo** (he/him) even lived there, Milan was a beacon of LGBTQ+ inclusivity in Italy—particularly in the now-renowned queer neighborhood of **Porta Venezia**.

"Centuries ago, Porta Venezia was the district with walls around it where people that had things like the Black Plague were put so they wouldn't infect other people outside those city walls. And for a long time, that district stayed a place for people who were not welcome or aligned with others in Milano," Daniele explained. "Slowly these people created a new, small neighborhood of their own in Porta Venezia—but the gay community was not the first that actually arrived there. The first was the Northern African community of Milano who moved there and started to open businesses in this place where no one wanted to go. Then the LGBTQ+ community arrived, and the magic of Milano made it happen that two different cultures—the queer community and people from Northern African countries that aren't usually friendly to the queer community—just started to talk to each other. They found a way to cohabitate in the same place, and they ended up creating the district of Porta Venezia as we know it today, which is now recognized as one of the best districts in the city of Milano."

It has been more than a decade since Daniele moved from the south of Italy to Milan, and more than two decades since his husband, Luigi, did the same. The two have called Milan's other up-and-coming queer district **NoLo** home since 2016—a year before they celebrated their wedding day in Milan, surrounded by family and friends.

Since they were wed in 2017, Luigi and Daniele have launched and led **Gayly Planet**—the first-ever travel blog for Italy's LGBTQ+ community—where they still share their insider knowledge about the best gay things to do in Milan, the rest of Italy, and beyond.

But as many destinations as they visit around the world, they are still proud to call Milan home. "Milano is the city where we met, so it's our place," Luigi said.

TO-DO LIST

"Milano is a unique city if you're looking for culture, because we have a large number of museums and galleries and places you can go to. The most-loved museum by the community is **Fondazione Prada**, a contemporary art museum housing Prada's own collection along with temporary exhibitions. There's also **Bar Luce** inside, which is a coffee shop that was designed by [US filmmaker] Wes Anderson. So, it's a beautiful place to go. You could spend half the day there.

"**Il Mudec** started as an anthropological museum, but it evolved into our museum of cultures. It explores different cultures from around around the world, and they have an exhibition that specifically explores culture in relation to genders, where contemporary artists from all the world have open discussions about how gender and gender roles are seen in different cultures. It's not a small gallery, it's a huge museum, but it's just perfection, because they're really committed to what they do there. And some of the exhibitions are free!

"If you are looking for books or gifts, especially books that talk about Milano from a queer perspective, there is a bookshop called **Antigone**. It's close to the Porta Venezia district and it's

one of our favorite places because you can find a treasure trove of different things, from photography books to hidden gems, targeted for queer readers."

EARLY MEALS

"The traditional breakfasts here are very sweet—a croissant or sponge cakes. To us, the best places to go for breakfast are just the local bars, because local-bar culture here is huge. They will always have pastries and coffee.

"For a posh breakfast, **Pasticceria Marchesi** is a historical spot founded by an Italian family called Marchesi 200 years ago, back in 1824. Now it's owned by the same group that owns Prada and there are three locations in Milan, but the original one is in the historical city center. It's known for having extremely high-quality coffee.

"We have a word for a specific type of people in Milano who are a part of our heritage: *sciura*. A *sciura* is like a wealthy, beautiful, elegant older woman who doesn't give a damn. So, if you want to feel like a *sciura*, just overdress, put on your nicest coat, add your finest jewelry, and go to Pasticceria Marchesi for breakfast.

"Another place for breakfast that is extremely local—we've never seen any tourists in there—and especially loved by the gay community is called **Pasticceria Sissi**. You can find very good croissants, brioche; very high-quality and so delicious. It's a local bar that is important to the community: old-style, not trendy but very popular.

"If you want to find good coffee, you can find it almost anywhere. But if you want to find the best quality, you have to look for *torrefazione*. These are coffee shops that own their own brand of coffee beans and use a very old, traditional method to roast them. Google *torrefazione* or ask around for them.

"We have this cultural thing for lunch in Italy but especially in Milano called **gastronomia**. It's like a small grocery shop—I think it's similar to the bodegas in New York—where they have a counter with many different kinds of foods. It can be sandwiches, meats, cheeses, but also lasagne and those kinds of things, that you can buy to eat there or take away to the park. Those *gastronomia* also have very high-quality dishes; you can find lobsters, risotto Milanese, all kinds of good food.

"There is one *gastronomia* we love called **La Madia**. It's very easygoing and they have some of the best lasagne, which is something that's unusual to find in a restaurant, but they also have ravioli and sandwiches. Otherwise, you can go to the best one close to the

Above: Pick up queer lit at Antigone, near Porta Venezia; Below: Lunchtime in Milan's Navigli neighborhood.

The More You Know

"We never sit. If you sit while you're having your coffee, you're either going to give someone bad news or really juicy gossip. So, we take our coffee at the counter."

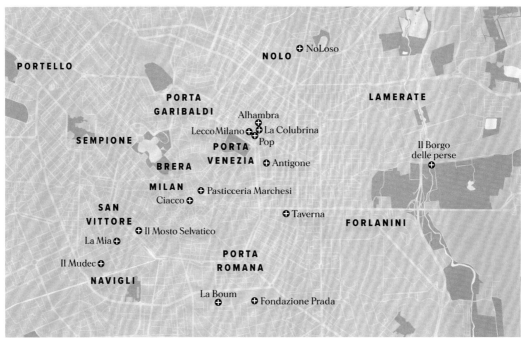

Duomo called **Peck**. It's one of the oldest *gastronomia* we have in Milano, since 1883. You can find everything you ever dreamed of eating there.

"There's a vegan place in Porta Venezia called **Alhambra**, which is an easygoing place with two buffets. We call them *tavola calda* and *tavola fredda*, the buffets, and they are not buffets like you would think of [at] other places. They're very common here. Alhambra is very cool and loved by the local queer community."

PIZZA & PASTA

"[There's] always time for pizza; any meal of the day. This isn't a local place, and it's not a secret—it's well-known—but it's called **Gino Sorbillo**. We love it so much. They have two locations in the historical center, which is nice because it can be difficult to find restaurants in the center that have high quality and good prices [but] that aren't a tourist trap. It's a good place, especially if you're short on time but you want to eat something extremely good, and don't want to pay a lot.

"Another pizza place that we love is **Il Mosto Selvatico**, which has only been open for a few years. Mostly they just do pizza, but elevated

Below: Pasta perfection in Milan;
Opposite: Cocktail time at Fondazione Prada's Bar Luce.

versions of pizza. It's a beautiful project dedicated to changing the district it's located in, which in the past was very dangerous. The pizza is absolutely perfection, and you know you are contributing to their project to continue improving the district. They also host events: live music, queer cabaret, performances from our local ballroom scene in their courtyard.

"**Taverna dei Terroni** is a very nice place inside the food market, but it's nothing fancy. It's absolutely the opposite of fancy. They have a little restaurant inside where the tables are covered with paper and it's very low-key, but you can go there for Sunday lunch. When our parents come to Milano we go there and have the exact same kind of experience we would have had at our own home.

"Pasta is more for lunch. There is a place that is very loved here called **miscusi**. There are a couple of restaurants with that same name and brand [that] are only here in Milano. They have very good pasta that is handmade daily. You can mix it with the sauce you want, and it's so delicious, and you can find locations in different parts of the city."

FIRST & SECOND DINNERS

"For tourists who are not used to having dinner late in the night, just know that actual dinnertime is not until around 9pm. We have our *aperitivo*, our Italian happy hour, around 6:30pm or 7pm, when you can order food and drinks, too. So, if you are not used to waiting until the Italian time for dinner—or to having a second dinner—just be prepared when you are traveling here.

"*Aperitivo* is, like, our religion. We live for *aperitivo*. We wait for *aperitivo* time to come every day. It's kind of like the tapas in Spain. You get your drink, then you can eat anything you want along with it. This is not just snacks like olives and nuts. *Aperitivo* can become almost like a proper dinner. You can find meat, pasta, risotto, pizza, and cakes.

"The place we love the most for *aperitivo*, which is also a queer place, is called **NoLoso**. It's in our district on the street that is becoming the new queer district. They have a pizzeria attached called **Gianni** that is from the same owner. Luigi *loves* and always orders the NoLo Reggo. It's one of their signature cocktails, made with gin, ginger, tabasco, pink pepper.

"**Osteria Memà** is an amazing Sicilian restaurant where you can always find different menus. The quality is over-the-top, and it's one of the best places you can go to find fine cuisine in a refined place, but a place that's still friendly.

"One of the best Milanese restaurants, which is actually vegetarian and vegan food, is **La Colubrina**. I went there without knowing that it was a vegan restaurant. The tiramisu here especially was so impressive; totally vegan and I would never have known it.

"For dessert: gelato. One of our favorite places close to the Duomo is called **Ciacco**. They have the best-quality gelato because they only use natural ingredients. The tip is to understand what good gelato actually looks like—if it's a giant pile of gelato in bright colors, we avoid it. Most of the gelato will be in the cone, if they do it right."

BARS & CLUBS

"There are many, many bars. [Porta Venezia] has two main streets for LGBTQ+ nightlife. One is **Via Lecco**, where there is the most popular bar, **LeccoMilano**. You can go there for *aperitivo*, you can go there after dinner, you can meet people.

"The other street, **Via Tadino**, is where you can find **Pop**, a trans-feminist bar, and it's very, very cool, especially for queer people who don't like the standard image of a gay nightlife. Everyone is welcome.

"We don't arrive at those types of places until one or two in the morning. On weekends, nightclubs don't even open until around midnight, and the night starts when the bars close. **La Boum** is very Milanese: fashion meets queer, with music from everywhere, but it's not pretentious.

"Then there is **Il Borgo delle perse**, and that's like a mix of *aperitivo* with a dance club with queer culture all mixed together. [It's] very chaotic, but if you love chaos, you're going to thrive there."

FIRST-TIMER TIPS

"People should know that a latte is a different thing than they think it is. A latte is just milk. You ask for an iced latte, they will give you cold milk, which is weird. If you really want something else—like how you think of a latte—it's a macchiato if you want more coffee than milk, or a latte macchiato if you want more milk than coffee.

"In a restaurant, we don't share. If we're there as a married couple, *maybe* we will exchange one slice of our pizza for a slice of the other's pizza, but that's because we're married—and even still, it can be exchanged, not shared.

"From 3pm, it's OK to drink at the bar. Not at a restaurant—you can drink earlier than that at a restaurant, with your lunch even. But [if] you go to the bar, you ask for prosecco or martini or your *aperitivo* at the counter, which is like with olives, and you have it there at the counter.

"Overall, take your time to walk around the Porta Venezia district to really take in the atmosphere. It is so full of different cultures, different flavors, and different people who found a way to live together peacefully."

Opposite: A vision in pink Candoglia marble, Milan's extravagant Gothic Duomo has presided over the city for some 600 years.

Stockholm,

SWEDEN

RECOMMENDATIONS BY

Lauren Aadland and Lisa Halling-Aadland

"I meant to visit her for just a couple of days in Stockholm, and I ended up staying a month," said **Lauren Aadland** (she/they/her/their) as she began telling the story of how she and her wife of 10 years, **Lisa Halling-Aadland** (she/her), first met.

"I said, 'I'm not going to do a long-distance relationship. So, if you want to be together, then you need to be working on getting your Swedish visa,'" Lisa said.

"And I said, 'All right,'" Lauren grinned.

Lauren's first month in Stockholm was in the dead of winter. "That was still very novel to me, the darkness and the snow. But we would still go out and do stuff. We'd go out to cozy cafes and have a glass of wine, nice meals. That was definitely a vibe I had never experienced before, being from California," Lauren said. "Then I saw Stockholm in the summertime and...the city just shook me."

Stockholm proper is spread across nine islands, while greater Stockholm is actually spread across 13 islands, so in the summertime, there's water everywhere. Lauren loved that they could swim in the Stockholm Archipelago right there in the city. But what they loved even more than the water was how welcomed they felt by everyone around them.

"That part of it was so magical. To walk around and feel how incredibly open and

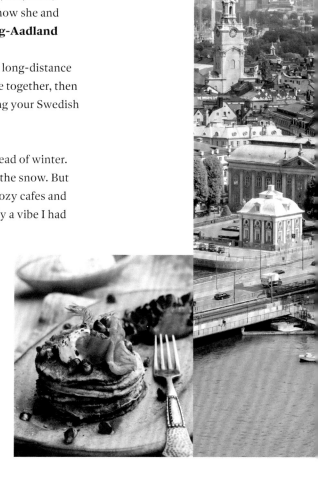

Below: A bird's eye view over Riddarholmen, Gamla Stan;
Opposite: Sample smoked-salmon pancakes and other Swedish delights in the city's renowned restaurants.

KNOW BEFORE YOU GO

....

LANGUAGE
Swedish

CURRENCY
Swedish Krona (kr, SEK)

PRIDE CELEBRATIONS
During the last week of July or
first week of August each year

WHEN TO GO
Between May and October for the
best weather/most sunshine

accepting the city is. It's like...you're safe any-where. You can go anywhere and be yourself. Nobody does double takes or anything like that," Lauren said. "There are so many people here just living their life, looking exactly how they want to look. Stockholm allows for a lot of safe creativity."

Lisa agreed: "Sweden has been really accept-ing of liberal views—politically but also socially and culturally—for so long," she said. "Now I think it's just kind of ingrained in our society. As a general rule of thumb for Stockholm and all of Sweden, it really is very accepting."

AN IDEAL DAY

"I would probably start at **Fotografiska**, which is a contemporary photo-art museum right on the water in Stockholm. It's amazing and also very boundary pushing. It's a lot of queer art in the contemporary sphere. They also have really good restaurants, sometimes live music.

"Then maybe we'd hop on a ferry cruise. All of these islands are connected—you can walk, there are bridges—but it's really nice, especially if it's hot out, to hop on one of the small ferries that takes you to the different islands.

"We could go over to an area called **Strand-vägen** for a nice, pretty, posh walk. There are so many cute little bars. There's a really nice cocktail bar there called **Glashuset**, which looks almost like a botanical garden, all encased in glass. I don't think they specifically call themselves a queer bar, but there happen to be a lot of gay people hanging out there. Strandvägen is also nice in the evening, when the sun begins to go down over the water.

"**Hallwylska Palace**, close to Strandvägen, was gifted from a family in Stockholm to the city of Stockholm in the early 1900s. It's a beautiful museum where they also do art exhi-bitions. Everything is completely preserved.

Above: Peruse the museum or enjoy a cocktail at grand Hallwylska Palace; ***Opposite:*** *Archipelago views from the bar at Fotografiska contemporary photo-art museum.*

They also have an upscale cocktail bar and lounge you can visit while you're there."

FIKA BREAK

"People would be upset if we didn't mention Swedish **fika**. *Fika* is basically a pause in the day to grab a cup of coffee and hang out for a little bit, and there's usually some type of little sweet roll involved. But it's more than just a cup of coffee. *Fika* is going and getting coffee and *conversing*. It's the act or experience of it, as opposed to what you're actually eating or drinking.

"There are two times in the day that you can do *fika*, around 10am and then around 3pm. It's a midmorning or midafternoon type of thing. With a visitor, we would go to **Gamla Stan**, which is a beautiful old town, and go up to the top to the very famous square **Stortorget** (the 'large square'). And on that large square is a famous queer cafe called **Chokladkoppen**, and they have delicious *fika*. Traditional Swedish would be a brewed coffee with a little chocolate ball or cinnamon bun. Another Swedish staple is *skagen*, a type of shrimp salad that is absolutely delicious and that you can find as a meal or appetizer pretty much everywhere.

"The microbrewery scene is popping, but at Swedish Christmas or *midsommar* you would have a little snaps. And this is not to be confused with German schnapps, which is actually sweet. This is not sweet. It's herbal, it's bitter, and it's strong, strong, strong. But you could definitely ask, 'Can I have a traditional Swedish snaps with my beer?' and they'll serve you something...well, probably disgusting, but it will be fun."

WINING, DINING & ABBA

"Walk around Gamla Stan. It's so beautiful there, and it's unlike any other place in Stockholm. There are shops and nice restaurants. **Bistro Pastis** is a French bistro, really small, but it's the cutest. It's down a narrow street, tucked in a corner.

"**Ulla Winbladh** is a restaurant that's been around for a long time; not overly expensive, but [with] high-quality, traditional Swedish dishes [made using] old recipes, and set in an old wood-and-stone villa. It's on the same island that a lot of the museums are on, but it's more of a locals' spot. In the winter it's cozy inside, and in the summer they have a huge patio. It feels fancy but it's accessible.

"It's near **ABBA: The Museum**, which is a go-to for the queer visitor. The **Vasa Museum** is right there too, which I think is a

The More You Know

"Just because there's not a rainbow flag somewhere does not mean it's not a welcoming space. You will see rainbow flags in some places. But if you see somewhere without one, it's probably just that the owner is like, 'Of course everyone is welcome here, it's Stockholm. Why would I need a flag in the window?'"

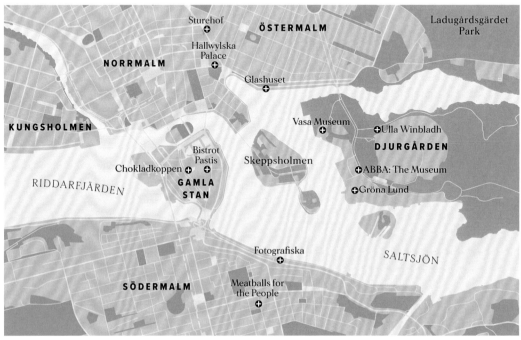

number-one attraction in Sweden. It's a 17th-century ship that sank something like a half-hour into its journey. They pulled the whole ship up so it's perfectly preserved, and they built a whole museum around it.

"There's a place called **Skansen** nearby, which is the open-air museum and wildlife reserve. The amusement park **Gröna Lund** is also right there.

"And then of course there's one of the world's largest sprawling art exhibitions, the **Stockholm subway system**. It's really fun. And that's definitely a thing that visitors do, go to specific stations to get pictures, especially Stadion, which has rainbow artwork.

"**Sturehof** is a classic restaurant that's been there for a long time. The kitchen is open late and the food is incredible. The later it gets, the more buzz there is in the restaurant. A small staircase takes you upstairs into a courtyard where there's a party with DJs and lights and a big bar, and it's always a party there. No admission fee, it's just a bar that turns into a party. And it's a good mix of

people. I don't even know if it has an official name, I think we just call it the **Courtyard**.

"There's a magazine called **QX** where they list everything LGBTQ+ that's going on in Stockholm. So, if you're particularly wanting to find a gay party, or whatever, look there."

FIRST-TIMER TIPS

"The south island, **Södermalm**, is definitely the queerest, hipster-iest area. It's a big island with lots of different neighborhoods to explore, with good, fun bars and nice restaurants. It's very fashionable and just a cool place to hang out. If you're on the west side of Södermalm, there's a restaurant called **Meatballs for the People**, for the Swedish meatballs you've been thinking about.

"I think a lot of people miss actually getting out on the water, whether it's kayaking or just getting on a cozy tour boat. There are a lot of tour boats that just run around the archipelago and you can get a glass of wine and sit and just relax. Once you cross the bridge from **Strandvägen** to **Djurgården**, to that island, there's a huge restaurant—a huge glasshouse-like cafe-restaurant; they also have paddleboats, little motorboats, stand-up paddleboards, kayaks, etc. You can start in a canal but then you can very easily make your way out to more open water if you want to."

*Right: Take time out over coffee and cinnamon buns in Swedish-fika style; **Opposite:** Alfresco dining in Stockholm's atmospheric Old Town.*

More Places to Visit

....

HERA	Patricia
HOPE STHLM	Side Track Bar & Restaurant
Mälarpaviljongen	The Blue Oyster
Moxy Stockholm	Urban Deli

Above: *The view to Vittoriosa from Triq San Gwann in Valletta.*

Valletta,
MALTA

RECOMMENDATIONS BY
Mina Jack Tolu

KNOW BEFORE YOU GO

. . . .

LANGUAGES
Maltese and
English

CURRENCY
Euro (€)

PRIDE CELEBRATIONS
Annually in
September

WHEN TO GO
In April or
October, to
avoid the heat
but still be
able to swim
comfortably

Malta consistently ranks in the top three most LGBTQ+-friendly countries in the world, and the most LGBTQ+-friendly country in Europe—thanks in no small part to Maltese locals like **Mina Jack Tolu** (they/he), a nonbinary transmasculine activist who has been fighting for queer and trans rights in their country for more than 15 years.

Mina Jack has lived in Sweden, Germany, Italy, and even the US for a stint. "It was eye-opening for me to be away from Malta," Mina Jack admitted. It's a small country, they explained, where a lot of people know each other—which can make exploring your gender and sexuality as a kid a little complicated.

"One of the first times I went to a gay bar in Malta, I bumped into a relative that I didn't even know was gay. These kind of awkward moments happen when you live in such a small place," Mina Jack said. "Living in Berlin for a few years after university allowed me the space to come out as nonbinary and trans, and to understand the kind of gender journey I wanted to be on."

But there were things back in Malta that Mina Jack missed too much to stay away for long. "One was my family, and another was the sea. As someone from an island, there's something beautiful about being within cycling distance of the sea," Mina Jack said. "I'd also done quite a bit of legwork as an activist to get Malta where we are today in terms of LGBTQI+ equality, and I wanted to be able to enjoy that."

While Mina Jack is proud of the progress Malta has made in terms of LGBTQI+ rights and acceptance, they don't think that a visit to Malta is necessarily the right choice for every gay traveler out there.

"Our beaches are not party beaches," Mina Jack said. "But if you're interested in culture, if you want to visit the Mediterranean but you're hesitant about visiting some of the more conservative countries where there's more homophobia, then Malta is a great place to come experience the beauty and the history of the region in a way that's safe for LGBTQI+ people."

WINING & DINING

"**Elephant Shoe** does amazing brunch, and it's friendly and gay-owned. When you walk in, there's a huge portrait of Bertha Saunders, also known as Katya Saunders. She's one of the first out trans women in Malta. When you're in the restaurant, you're kind of seated with Bertha/Katya.

"**Cafe Society** is more for evening vibes. They have nice cocktails, they organize drag and burlesque shows, they have DJs, sometimes they're exhibiting queer artists. The bar itself is very small but patrons take over the steps outside. It's got a big rainbow flag outside—you can't miss it—and it overlooks the **Grand Harbour**.

"A bit further south, there's **Ġugar Hangout & Bar**, which is a vegetarian cafe that's very queer-friendly. You can buy local music there, local CDs (and cassettes, for some reason), and tote bags. The food is very good, and the beer's cold. You can sit on the steps in the street and you know you're going to be welcome.

"Just a stone's throw away is **Maori**, one of the biggest supporters of the LGBTQI+ community and organizers in Malta. It's a bar-slash-event venue, right on the sea. I really feel at home when I go there. In the summer, it's a nice place to go after a swim. It's a really important place for the LGBTQI+ community, and owner Simone loves meeting new people and travelers who come by.

"There's usually a lesbian party event somewhere in Malta every two months, either a WLW [women-loving women] event like **Peach** or a more queer party like **Nerve**. Around every six weeks, there's another one called **Lollipop**, which is welcoming to the whole queer community."

Above: Valletta's queer-friendly Ġugar Hangout & Bar, top stop for local music and meat-free meals; Below: Sunny skies over the Mediterranean in storied Valletta.

ARTS & CULTURE

"My top recommendation would be the **megalithic temples: Ġgantija**, **Ħaġar Qim**, **Mnajdra**, **Skorba**, **Ta' Ħaġrat**, and **Tarxien**. They were built—we don't know quite how—around 3000 to 6000 BCE. They're even older than Stonehenge, and Ħaġar Qim and Mnajdra in particular are up on the cliffs, so you get this dramatic view of them against the sea. It's really special.

"**Spazju Kreattiv** is in Valletta. It's a gallery space, but they also have the only art-house cinema in Malta, and they're very conscious about including queer films in their programming, including queer films that tour European film festivals. It's very affordable, too, less than €10 per ticket. It's a very small cinema, very cute. And in summer, sometimes you do just want to sit in an air-conditioned room and watch a movie. Then by the time you leave, it's dark outside and it's cooler, and you can go for drinks somewhere nearby in Valletta. It's that kind of vibe.

"There's a store called **il-lokal** which has artwork by Maltese artists and artists living in Malta, including some by LGBTQI+ artists. They're very friendly and always happy to help people find the right print or piece of pottery or notebook or so on. There's also **Storeroom**, which is a music bar. About once a month, there's a drag show there, and it's only like 5km [3 miles] from Valletta.

"**Rosa Kwir** is a trans-owned gallery operated by a Maltese contemporary artist. It's the first LGBTQI+ gallery and archive in Malta. It's beautiful. Sometimes they host music nights, open-mic nights, poetry, exhibitions, and parties as well."

GETTING OUTDOORS

"My favorite place to get out of the urban center of Malta is in the north: **Il-Majjistral Nature and History Park**. Majjistral is actually Malta's first natural national park. It's a protected **Natura 2000 Site**, which is one of the protections at a European level for rare natural habitats and species. It's a great place for a hike. You'll see carob, a flowering shrub that's been in Malta for centuries. If you're very quiet, you hear seabirds.

"The smells are beautiful, too. I love walking through Majjistral because you smell thyme and carob, and you smell the salt in the air from the sea. For me, that's the smell of Malta: the smell of thyme and carob and salty sea air, especially in the summer.

"Close to Majjistral, there's a bay called **Għajn Tuffieha**, which has a great beach. You're surrounded by greenery, and once you're down there—except for the little restaurant they built—you don't see any buildings or construction, you don't hear any traffic."

LOCAL EATS

"One of the most famous Maltese dishes is *pastizzi*, which is like a flaky pastry filled with cheese—ricotta, usually—and peas, like mushy peas. You can find those everywhere, and they're like 50 cents.

"We always tell people to try Kinnie, which is a soft drink. It's fizzy, and it's kind of a bitter orange taste. Kinnie sponsors Pride here, too, and they come out with different Pride merch every year.

"**Bohini** on the north of the island is a lesbian-owned restaurant with great vegetarian options, local **Lot 61** coffee, good tea. They also make their own strawberry jam with fresh Mġarr strawberries that you can buy. One note: they don't allow anyone under 18."

GETTING AROUND THE ISLAND

"If you're staying in Valletta, the buses are actually really convenient. Otherwise, rideshares would be safe. You can also book

The More You Know

"Nudity is not typically allowed. It's illegal to be topless in Malta anywhere other than the beach—unless you have boobs, in which case it's always illegal to be topless. Even on a hot day in the middle of Malta, the police have been known to stop anyone who is topless, so do be careful."

Above: *Taking a break from the heat in Valletta;* ***Opposite:*** *Evening drinks on Valletta's Strait St.*

Storeroom ✛

Maori ✛   Ġugar Hangout
          ✛ and Bar
VALLETTA
il-lokal ✛

Spazju Kreattiv ✛   ✛ Cafe Society
                     ✛ Elephant Shoe

FLORIANA

GRAND HARBOUR

SENGLEA
          VITTORIOSA

MEDITERRANEAN SEA

Il-Majjistral Nature
✛ and History Park
✛ Għajn Tuffieħa

   ✛ Bohini
MGARR

            Rosa Kwir   See enlargement
               ✛   ┌─ ─ ─ ─ ─
MDINA   Malta   **VALLETTA**
RABAT   └─ ─ ─ ─ ─
            ŻEBBUĠ   **COSPICUA**

                         ŻEJTUN

         Ħaġar Qim
            ✛   **BIRŻEBBUĠA**

cabs that have female drivers for a little extra fee on a local rideshare called **eCabs** with their Women+ feature.

"You can take the **fast ferry** that takes 45 minutes to **Gozo**, but if it's windy and you're not good with seasickness, you don't want to do that. The slower ferries within the harbor cross from Valletta to the **Three Cities**: **Vittoriosa**, **Senglea**, and **Cospicua**. Or you can cross over to **Sliema**, which is cafes, bars, malls, big hotels. It still has an old urban center, but it's much more urbanized. **Kaktus Cafe** is a great spot to check out in Sliema, too. It's owned by queer migrants."

FIRST-TIMER TIPS

"In Valletta, keep quiet after 11pm. There are residents, many of them elderly, who have lived there their entire lives. After 11pm, they might even call the police on you if you're too loud.

"If something happens to you—if you're discriminated against, or you're a victim of homophobia, hate speech, violence—do go to the police, but also call local organizations or get in touch with a local activist, because we'll be able to assist you with the report. Reach out to an organization like **Malta LGBTQI+ Rights Movement** (MGRM; maltagayrights.org) or **Allied Rainbow Communities** (gaymalta.com). If the issue is discrimination based more on ethnicity or racism, MGRM is the better one to contact.

"Come here if you want to go on a cultural holiday that connects you to a very important place historically for the Mediterranean, if you want to understand colonization and what a post-colonial island of the UK looks like. We've gone through British rule, Arabic rule, Spanish rule, and there's so much to learn about the influence of all of these cultures on our architecture, our language, our cuisine, everything here. It's a unique place to explore."

Anchorage,
USA

RECOMMENDATIONS BY

Justine and Sam Goldon

When **Justine Goldon** (she/her) first met **Sam Goldon** (they/them), they'd both moved from their home states—Virginia and Alaska, respectively—to live in Denver, Colorado.

"Living in Colorado was great, but I raved about Alaska. I was pretty bratty about it," Sam said. "We'd be somewhere pretty in Colorado and I'd be like, 'Yeah, it's OK, but it's no Alaska.'"

"And I'd be like, 'It's beautiful, what are you talking about? You sound like an asshole!'" Justine laughed. "And then we went to Alaska for a visit and I was like, 'Oh, OK, I get it now.'"

But as a teenager in Alaska, Sam's experience wasn't quite so beautiful. "I grew up in a very conservative home a little outside of Anchorage in a very white, conservative, Mormon, Christian community. At that point, I felt like the only queer person in Alaska. I felt very alone," Sam said. "But we were so pleasantly surprised since moving back to Anchorage as adults to find that the queer community here is actually thriving!"

Sam and Justine are now proud to call Anchorage their forever home—both because of the community they've found there and the natural beauty the area has to offer.

"The outdoors, especially in a place like Alaska, is just so healing and liberating. As a queer person, as a trans person, to be able to access that and be immersed in that is incredible,"

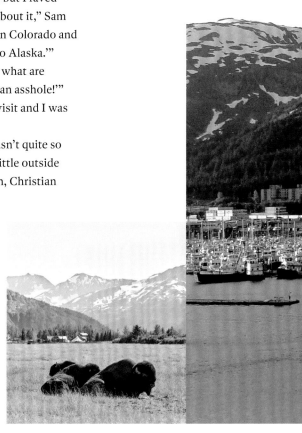

Below: On the edge of the wilderness in Whittier, just south of Anchorage; *Opposite:* Bison at the Alaskan Wildlife Conservation Center on the scenic Seward Hwy.

Sam said. "Nature is a safe space for everybody. It's accepting of us all. That's such a beautiful thing, and a lot of people don't have access to that. I think that's part of what makes this place so special in general, but for queer people especially."

TO CRUISE OR NOT TO CRUISE

"From an accessibility perspective, taking a cruise can be a really cool way for an older person, a family, or a disabled person to experience the beauty of Alaska safely. What we love so much about Alaska is getting out into the backcountry, which a cruise doesn't necessarily give you the time or space to do.

"Anchorage, and Alaska as a whole, is not somewhere you can just spend a day or two. You need four or five days at least, because that allows you to do a backpacking trip, which is two days in itself already. That allows you to have a decompression day, it gives you time to get to one of the seaside areas or to do a day trip, because there's so much to see and do while you're here."

AN IDEAL DAY

"In downtown Anchorage we have a queer-friendly place called **K Street Market**, which is like a little co-op building with multiple businesses in it. There's **Fire Island Rustic Bakeshop**, which is incredible, and that's connected to **That Feeling Co**, which is a shop with plants and gifts and incredible coffee—super queer, cool, and funky. Then in the same market you can find **Johnny's Produce** for smoothies, juices, local produce, lots of Alaskan-made goods. And that's connected to **La Bodega**, a small wine-and-spirits store with lots of cool local brews, mocktail options, things like that.

"Then we're going to get our sandwiches from Fire Island to go, and we're heading outdoors.

*Above: Mushers on the move during the legendary Iditarod dog-sled race from Anchorage to Nome; **Opposite**: Queer-friendly That Feeling Co at Anchorage's K Street Market.*

"If it's winter, learning to cross-country ski here is amazing. **Hatcher Pass** has a great cross-country skiing area at **Archangel Road** in winter, and there are these adorable little red huts you can rent at **Hatcher Pass Lodge**, which still looks straight out of the '70s and they have no intention of updating it. They have a sauna, and it's on a little creek, so you can do a sauna and then a cold plunge. They have live music, you can get an amazing view of the Northern Lights in the winter, and it's affordable.

"But Hatcher Pass in the summertime is one of our favorite places, too. It feels like Narnia. We love to hike **Reed Lakes** in the summer, which is about a 6-mile [10km] round-trip. You see beautiful turquoise lakes, the jagged mountains, and everything is green.

"On our way back to town from Hatcher Pass, , we'll call ahead to place a pizza order from **Moose's Tooth Pizza**, because—especially if it's summertime—the wait will be long. They serve more pizza per capita than any pizzeria in the United States! We'll go there, have a beer, sit by the fire, then eat. They have reindeer sausage and other local specialties. They also have their own brewery connected to the restaurant.

"Then we'll go to **Wild Scoops**, the best local ice-cream shop with a lot of cool flavors, because the foraging here in Alaska is phenomenal—blueberries, lots of fireweed—and they incorporate all of these local ingredients into their ice creams. Our freezer is full of salmon, halibut, and Wild Scoops."

QUEER-OWNED

"**Mad Myrna's** is a long-standing pillar of the LGBTQ+ community in Anchorage. It's the one real gay bar here. They have amazing dancing, drag nights, and it's a really fun vibe.

"**Rage City Vintage** is a queer consignment and vintage shop that hosts events each week, too—all kinds of stuff, ranging from Lego-building nights to 'Stitch and Bitch' sessions for knitters, and other eclectic events like live music and art shows.

"There's a tropical fusion restaurant called **Palmeria** that's queer-owned and also hosts drag and burlesque events. There's also a place called **Gather Alaska** in town that's queer-owned and offers yoga.

"**Arciniega Street Productions** hosts queer-focused pop-up events in different spaces around Anchorage. They do a quarterly show called **Vibes**, which is a burlesque drag show. Then they host all-ages events that are sober-friendly, like **Drag Lotería**. They do

The More You Know

"We don't want to be like, 'Be scared of bears!' but really, you have to carry bear spray, and you have to have it accessible and know how to use it. Make sure you educate yourself before you come up here—the difference between black bears and brown bears, what to do for each. And moose, too."

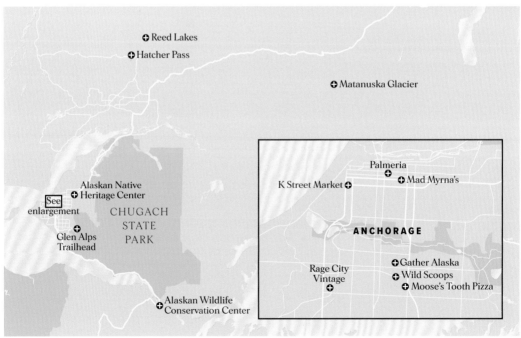

a lot of dry events, too, with mocktails because there's a big queer-sober scene in Alaska.

"Alaska is like, a decade behind on technology. So, Facebook is still how most people communicate here. There is a Facebook group called **Queer Happenings Alaska**, where all of the events happening in Anchorage are posted and where people will be like, 'I'm queer, I'm visiting, I want to go on a hike, does anyone want to come?'"

GETTING OUTDOORS

"In the wintertime, they have two main trail systems in Anchorage, and they're lit up at nighttime. As soon as it's dark outside, they're lit. And there are [also] lit, groomed ski trails that are free and accessible to the public any time. And this network of mountains—we could mountain-bike from our house to anywhere.

"Another huge thing about Alaska is all the public-use cabins that you can book. There are so many! We'll have friends come visit and we'll tie sleds to ourselves and cross-country ski to a cabin in the wilderness. So, we have these little queer

*Below: Immerse in the wilderness at Hatcher Pass Lodge; **Opposite:** Alaska's backcountry is a haven for wildlife—including brown bears.*

weekend retreats with our friends, huddling over woodstoves, melting snow for water. It's magical.

"If you want to hike into the **Chugach Mountains**, the **Glen Alps Trailhead** is a good place to start. If you're coming up and you don't have outdoorsy gear, you can rent from **Out Yonder Camping Co**. They're a queer-owned outdoor-gear rental company. So, if you wanted to rent a 4WD vehicle or a rooftop tent or anything, they have that kind of stuff available, which is really cool.

"Get to a glacier. You gotta see a glacier when you come to Alaska. We take people to **Matanuska Glacier**, where you can pay for a tour to walk on, in, and around the actual glacier. They teach you all about the layers of ice, and you can even crawl through the glacier. Definitely go on a weekday if you can, because the weekend tour groups can get quite large. If you're with an Alaska resident, the tour is half price, so make a friend in the community and see if they want to go to Matanuska with you."

NATIVE LAND

"So much of Alaska is still made up of Native villages, and we're very much living on Native land. Anchorage is in **Dena'ina Ełnena**, the traditional homeland of the **Dena'ina Athabascan** people. So, when you're here, please be respectful of the land, and be respectful of Indigenous communities.

"There's an organization called **Native Movement** that provides a lot of resources and education around Alaska's Native community, and that's definitely something I think people should review before they come here. Once you're here, the **Alaskan Native Heritage Center** is phenomenal, with a beautiful exhibit on Alaskan Native culture.

"Another place we take people is the **Alaskan Wildlife Conservation Center**. It's down along

the **Seward Hwy**. A lot of these animals are in rehabilitation and will be released as soon as it's safe to do so. They do really great work there, and they offer educational resources about the wildlife in Alaska. And it's beautiful! There's a mountain behind you while you're looking at all these moose and caribou, and it's so cool to see."

FIRST-TIMER TIPS

"Public transportation isn't really a thing here. You're going to want to rent a car.

"Respect wildlife, and leave no trace. Be prepared on the trails, and recognize that if you're putting yourself in danger and expecting other people to help you if you get stuck, you're also putting them in danger.

"Before you go on a hike, make sure you check the **Hiking in Alaska** Facebook group to see if the trail conditions are safe. You don't want to end up somewhere with overgrown conditions where you can't see wildlife, or other dangerous conditions that could put you at risk.

"But overall, the thing that makes Alaska different is that the people who live here or come here really have to want to. It's a rugged lifestyle in a lot of ways, and you have to rely on your community for things. We're here because we love it here. And the people that come to visit want to love it here and experience that, too. And you really feel that in the vibe of Anchorage, particularly within the queer community. You'll be embraced here."

Above: *Perfect peak views on the Flattop Mountain Trail, an easy day-hike right from central Anchorage.*

Above: *Perfect conditions for paddling at Lady Bird Lake.*

Austin,
USA

RECOMMENDATIONS BY

Sam Slupski

KNOW BEFORE YOU GO

LANGUAGE
English

CURRENCY
USD ($)

PRIDE CELEBRATIONS
Annually in
early August

WHEN TO GO
During
shoulder season
(March–June
or September–
November)
to avoid the
summer heat

Lauded as one of the most LGBTQ+-friendly cities in the United States and proud of its unofficial city motto 'Keep Austin Weird'; it's no wonder that the Texan capital continues to act as a safe haven for queers in the American South.

Although queer, trans, nonbinary writer **Sam Slupski** (they/them) originally hails from the Midwest, after graduating from college they found themself among the many folks in the LGBTQ+ community who couldn't resist Austin's siren song.

"I visited Austin a lot in my early 20s and was always so struck by how beautiful and green it was," Sam said. "I was really drawn to the outdoor activities in the city but, ultimately, I decided to move to Austin because of the literary and poetry community here."

Sam was quick to note that Texas isn't queer-friendly on the whole as a state. "There are people and politicians here who are so staunch in their homophobia and transphobia that it can feel really scary to travel through parts of this state," they said. "There have been over 30 anti-trans bills that have been introduced into the legislation in this state alone."

But as a consistently blue (liberal) city in a sea of red (conservative) regions, Sam said Austin still feels like a place where the queer community is warmly welcomed and where LGBTQ+ locals show up for each other.

"The people in Austin overall really do protect one another. I have seen that firsthand through protests, events, and in my own circles," Sam said. "There are so many businesses here that have absolutely no tolerance for hate and bigotry. And if someone does experience something that feels harmful when they're out somewhere, people are quick to shut the behavior down and make it known that that place isn't one to be supported."

QUEER SPRINKLES

"There is the queer-bar street, which is **4th St**. However, if you're not looking for alcohol-centered activities, there are queer-friendly spaces sprinkled throughout the city.

"There are also so many queer events here, like the **Greetings from Queer Mountain: Queer Storytelling** series, events put on by **Future Front**, and drag brunch at **Coconut Club** on Saturdays. You can also check out **@localqueeratx**, **@queerswimatx**, **@queercraftclub**, **@queerfriendsatx**, and **@queersoberatx** on Instagram for a bunch of different queer events and meetups in the city."

AN IDEAL DAY

"My ideal 24 hours in Austin would start with breakfast on the patio at **Proud Mary**, where my partner and I are regulars. I always get the potato hash, the hotcakes, and try one of their unique [coffee] pour-overs that rotate out seasonally.

"From there, I'd probably go to **Mills Pond** to go birding. But if I didn't want to make the trek north for birding, I'd head to East Austin and do some shopping at **Little Gay Shop**, **Tillery Street Plant Company**, **Take Heart**, and then **Howdy's Vintage**.

"I'd either get lunch at **La Santa Barbacha** for tacos or go get takeout at **Little Deli** and head to

Above: Green shopping at Tillery Street Plant Company;
Below: Indulging in down-home Texas barbecue is an Austin essential.

Pease Park for a little picnic. Then I'd eventually get an afternoon caffeine boost at **Fleet Coffee**, where the baristas are always amazing.

"I'd either go take a dip at **Deep Eddy Pool** and get dinner at **Pool Burger**, or I'd get a little dressed up to get drinks at **Kinda Tropical** or **LoLo**. If there was an outdoor drag show at **Cheer Up Charlies** and I had the energy, I'd consider going."

WEEKEND PLANS

"Friday: grab drinks and tacos at **Cosmic Saltillo** for an early dinner and then go to **Zilker Park** to watch the **Zilker Summer Musical**. If musicals aren't your thing, head to **Hotel Vegas** or **Chess Club** to see some live music. Or visit the **South Congress Bridge** to see the famous bats at sunset.

"Saturday: wake up early to get a table at **Paperboy** in East Austin. If you end up having to wait for a table, walk around and check out all the little shops East Austin has to offer. My favorites are **LoveCraft**, **Apartment F**, and **Charm School Vintage**.

"Get a latte to go at **Paperboy** and go walk the **Trail at Lady Bird Lake**. Make sure to stop at **Lou Neff Point** for a beautiful view of the skyline. After, grab lunch at **Soup Peddler**, where they have the best smoothies in town, and then make your way north to check out **Side Kitsch Vintage**, **BookWoman**, **Top Drawer Thrift**, and **Okasan Vintage**. If you want to keep the vintage shopping going, walk over to **North Loop** and stop at **Room Service Vintage**. If you're feeling something more low-key, go to **Little Gay Shop** for a queer treat and check out what gallery show is happening at **Prizer Arts and Letters**.

"Before you go to whatever local queer event you find, grab a quick dinner at **Home Slice Pizza** from their takeout window. Then after the event,

The More You Know

"We gotta be real: it's Texas. But while Texas may not be queer-friendly on the whole as a state, Austin feels like a place where the queer community really shows up for one another."

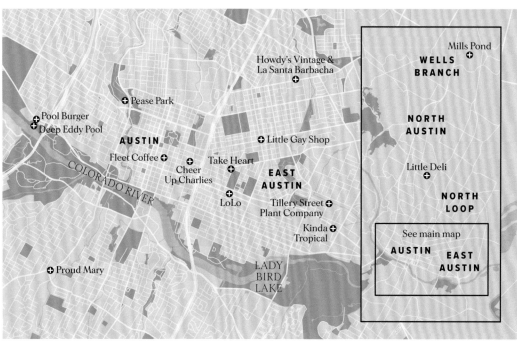

head to **Holiday** for cocktails or a mocktail for a nightcap.

"Sunday: get a coffee at **Fleet on Manor** followed by breakfast tacos at **La Santa**. Pop by **Howdy's** for some vintage shopping and then check out **Laguna Gloria** or **Mayfield Park** before you have to leave for the airport or get on the road."

THE GREAT OUTDOORS

"Walk around **Town Lake Trail** and stop by one of the many boat rentals and grab a kayak or canoe for a couple of hours. Get some good views at **Mt Bonnell** or the **Pennybacker Bridge**. Go birding at **Hornsby Bend** or **Mills Pond**. Go swimming at **Deep Eddy** or **Barton Springs**. Hike one of the many greenbelts, such as **Barton Creek**, **St Edwards**, **Bull Creek**, or **Onion**

Below: Breakfast on the patio at Proud Mary; ***Opposite:*** *Ambling Austin's South Congress.*

Creek. Check out **Wild Basin Wilderness Preserve**. Go to **Lady Bird Johnson Wildflower Center**. Take a day trip to **Wimberley**. Check out **Blue Hole Regional Park**."

ROMANTIC RENDEZVOUS

"Get a tandem kayak and take some time on **Lady Bird Lake** to take in the nature of Austin. Stay at **Carpenter Hotel**, where you never have to leave because they have a coffee shop, restaurant, and a swimming pool for guests. Get reservations at **Equipment Room**, which is an awesome bar on **South Congress** that is really dark and romantic, spins vinyl with a high-quality, yet chill sound, and order a couple of their unique cocktails. Go to **Justine's** or **Prélude** for beautiful dinner and drinks."

WINING, DINING & BOATING

"Grab reservations at **Launderette**, **Hestia**, or **Suerte**. Get drinks at **Holiday**, **Kitty Cohen's**, **Mama Dearest**, **La Holly**, **Nickel City**, or **Kinda Tropical**. Book a **Retro Boat Rentals** and take in the Austin skyline."

Brooklyn,
USA

RECOMMENDATIONS BY

Regennia Johnson and Melinda Murillo

When couple **Regennia 'Gennia' Johnson** (she/her) and **Melinda 'Lenny' Murillo** (she/her) met in a bar back in their home state of Oklahoma, only one of them knew that they'd move to the Big Apple one day.

While Oklahoma City–born Gennia was used to the hustle and bustle of urban life, she always wanted to live in an even bigger city—specifically, New York City. On the flip side, Lenny came from a small Oklahoma town called Guthrie and had never had an interest in city living.

"At first, I was kind of afraid to live in New York," Lenny admitted. "But Regennia shed light on some of the pros, the biggest of them being community. And I could see how it would be good for us, as a same-sex couple, to be around more people from the LGBTQ+ community. And in the end, it was a good choice for us. Now I want to live here for the rest of my life."

The two moved to **Bedford-Stuyvesant** (aka **Bed-Stuy**), in north-central Brooklyn. "Brooklyn as a whole is historically Black, and that's true of Bed-Stuy, especially," Gennia said. "It's a wonderful community and a thriving neighborhood, and we knew that's where we wanted to be. Being Black is a huge part of our identity, and when I think about the places where we spend our time and the businesses we support, as often as possible those are owned and

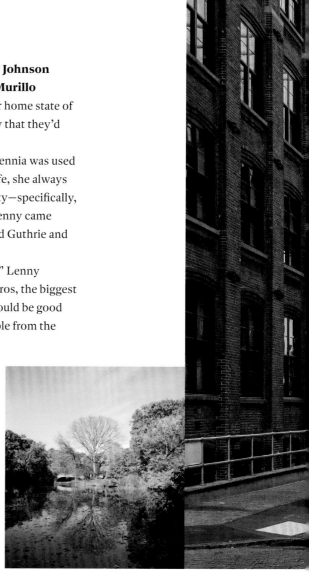

Below: Manhattan Bridge from Washington St in Brooklyn's Dumbo district; **Opposite:** *Fall colors in Prospect Park.*

operated by Black women and women of color. Maybe they're not LGBTQ+-owned specifically, but they're always LGBTQ+-friendly."

"Bed-Stuy, Brooklyn, really all of New York, is so LGBTQ+-friendly," Lenny added. "You don't necessarily need to go out and find dedicated queer spaces because even if a place isn't LGBTQ+ owned and operated, it's likely still friendly to the community and welcoming to the people in it."

A couple of years later, Lenny and Gennia agree: moving from Oklahoma to Brooklyn was one of the best decisions they've ever made. "We absolutely love living here, and we love our community," Gennia said. "We've got our church and our church family, our close-knit group of friends who are like our chosen family. Why would we ever want to leave this?"

AN IDEAL DAY

"We'd start our day at the park. Right in our neighborhood here in **Bed-Stuy** is **Herbert Von King Park**. It's a cute little park, definitely not as big as **Prospect Park** in Brooklyn or anything, but it's our neighborhood park. It also has the **Herbert Von King Dog Run**, so we like to bring our dog there. And it has this nice grassy area where we like to sprawl out, and in the afternoons there'll sometimes be a DJ there. Might have some families there hanging out. We always see same-sex couples there, too, just sitting and people-watching.

"After that, we'll probably get coffee at **BKLYN BLEND**. It's a Black-owned cafe; sometimes people will come and play some live music. There's also a little coconut shop right next door, where this guy serves fresh natural coconuts for a living—that's poppin' in the summer.

"For lunch, we like to eat at **Peaches**: really good Southern food—fried catfish, fried chicken, all of that. Then after that, there's also an

ice-cream spot near there called **Brown Butter Creamery**, right on **Tompkins** [Ave].

"For dinner, we like **Pattie Hut & Grill**, which is a Caribbean spot, but it's only to-go.

"Honestly, after that, we would probably just stumble into something, like places hosting pop-up events."

SHOPPING AROUND

"There's a bookstore called **The Word is Change** in Bed-Stuy. The same goes for **Cafe Con Libros**, a bookstore and cafe nearby in **Crown Heights**.

"**Sincerely, Tommy** is a Black-owned, LGBTQ+-friendly boutique. The woman who owns it is deeply rooted in Bed-Stuy. Her family owns a couple of places in the neighborhood. The family is really interwoven into the fabric of the neighborhood and the community. They have clothes and accessories in their boutique...serve coffee...it's a neighborhood staple.

"**Peace & RIOT** is a cute Black-owned shop with all kinds of different knickknacks: coffee-table books, home decor items, games. You could find a gift for just about anybody there."

GETTING ACTIVE

"Lenny likes to go to the **Brooklyn Community Pride Center Bed-Stuy** for pickup basketball games. They have different events centered around community and mindfulness. All you have to do is RSVP to attend, and sometimes there's a cost but sometimes they're free. They have a skate night, a swim night, and more, and you can just drop in."

Gennia has also tried **OutBox** in Williamsburg: "[It's] a transowned and operated gym and fitness facility that has some great inclusive fitness offerings."

LOCAL NIGHTLIFE

"The **Bush** is a bar that later at night can be like a club situation, with dancing and a DJ. But it's more of a bar, with good drinks where you can hang out and talk to people. They also host a ton of events.

"**Raw Honey** is an organization that curates events and different kinds of parties, not just nightlife but all kinds of events like day parties, trivia, karaoke, things like that. **Funky Reggae House Party** is another event curator we follow, with some really great

Above: Manhattan views from the Brooklyn Bridge Park;
Opposite: Club goers wait in line outside of Elsewhere nightclub.

DJs. **Elsewhere** is an awesome venue that hosts a lot of LGBTQ+ events. So does the **Bogart House**.

"Before you show up at an event, be cognizant of who you are and what type of space you are occupying. Double-check if it's somewhere that you should bring your straight friend along, and see if they have rules or guidelines to follow."

HISTORY & CULTURE

"There's the **Weeksville Heritage Center**, where the first Black community was in Brooklyn. We have the **Brooklyn Museum**, **Brooklyn Academy of Music**, and the **Brooklyn Children's Museum**.

"Our church, **Bethany Baptist Church**, has been in establishment for 140 years, since 1883. One of our friends who is queer is actually a minister and a leader in that church. We've never felt unwelcome there. We've always felt very embraced and encouraged and included in the conversations."

The More You Know

"Normally we wouldn't take the subway after midnight. If it gets that late, we're gonna go ahead and Uber just to keep things safe. Because it's like people say, very late at night and very early in the mornings is when stuff happens."

Above: Take in music, dance or a movie at the Brooklyn Academy of Music; *Opposite:* Marsha P Johnson Park in Williamsburg.

OutBox

Bogart House

LIAMSBURG

Elsewhere

The Bush

BUSHWICK

BKLYN BLEND

Herbert Von King Park

Sincerely, **BEDFORD-**
Tommy **STUYVESANT**

Butter Creamery &
The Word is Change ◆ peace & RIOT

Pattie Hut & Grill

Brooklyn
ommunity Pride
Center Bed-Stuy **BROOKLYN**

Cafe Con Libros

CROWN HEIGHTS

GETTING OUTSIDE

"**Riis Beach** is a super-popular beach, especially with the LGBTQ+ community. Some people don't realize that New York has beaches, but it's such a cool place and not far at all to get to. And we love **Marsha P Johnson Park** in Williamsburg, right on the water."

FIRST-TIMER TIPS

"If there's any place that you really can just wear whatever you want, it's New York. I feel like my style is elevated in New York, because I come outside and I see people wearing things that I'm like: 'Wow!' I would never have thought to put that together, but it looks so nice.

"Be aware of your surroundings. You can be on your phone, trying to make sure you're going the right way and following directions, but stay aware.

"Regardless of what you might think, people know each other in New York. People take care of each other. There are a lot of shitty things happening, but there are also good things. And we appreciate that about Brooklyn, especially about the queer community and the Black community in Brooklyn."

More Places to Visit

....

Early Yves

Risbo

Cups and Books

Club Lamda BK

L'imprimerie

Lesbian Herstory Archives

Mary's Bar Brooklyn

Paradise Taco

Superfine

Above: *Sunset over the city from the Portland Aerial Tram.*

Portland,
USA

RECOMMENDATIONS BY
Charlie Sprinkman

KNOW BEFORE YOU GO

LANGUAGE
English

CURRENCY
USD ($)

PRIDE CELEBRATIONS
Annually
in June

WHEN TO GO
Summer for
warm, dry
weather;
shoulder season
(March–May
or September–
November)
for mild
temperatures
and fewer
crowds

As they road-tripped solo through 41 of the 50 United States, **Charlie Sprinkman** (he/they) found themself returning to Google to search 'queer spots in [enter city and state here]' again and again to no avail.

"I said, 'I just wish there was a map of safe spaces for queer people,' and the lightbulb lit up," Charlie recounted. From that point on, they couldn't stop ruminating on this idea. So just a few months later, **Everywhere Is Queer** was born.

"As someone who grew up in rural America and was raised conservative and Catholic, I wanted to create something that would allow the queer, trans, and ally community to navigate the world locally or globally as their true, authentic selves, all while supporting entrepreneurs in the community," Charlie explained.

The innovative and inclusive (and free!) Everywhere Is Queer app that Charlie created makes it easy to find more than 15,000 welcoming, LGBTQ+-owned spaces to shop, connect, eat, learn, and grow all over the world—and of course, in your own hometown, too. They have created a Job Board front and center in-app to allow users to find jobs that see themselves as their most authentic self.

"There are more than 675 queer-owned businesses on the Everywhere Is Queer map in Portland alone," Charlie said of the Oregon city they call home. "My partner and I walk the streets of Portland holding hands and we're constantly waving to another queer couple, then another queer couple, then another queer couple."

While there's a lot Charlie loves about Portland, the fact that the whole city is so welcoming and safe for LGBTQ+ locals and visitors alike is at the top of the list. "Portland feels like I live in a queer commune," they said. "There's no queer neighborhood, it's just the whole city of Portland."

AN IDEAL DAY

"In the morning, go and get a smoothie from **Poppy's Smoothie Cart** outside of the **People's Food Co-op**.

"I love Southeast Portland. That's where I choose to live. There's so much to do between **Division, Hawthorne,** and **Belmont** [streets]. So many amazing places, and you don't even need a car or a bike.

"**Gone West PDX** is a queer-owned plant shop, just a really cute store if you ever need a gift for someone or want to treat yourself. **Hello**

Sunshine Art + Vintage is a fun vintage store up on Belmont, just a little bit north, with a great clothing selection. **Honeyed Words** is a local independent bookstore that hosts book signings and other cool events. **Daffodill Studios** is an awesome studio offering ceramics classes and art classes, and anyone can drop in. **Seagrape Apothecary** has all things wellness, herbs... that sort of thing.

"And the food scene is just crazy out here. Endless possibilities. There are food-truck pods around every corner; one I always recommend, that was established by queer people and where all the trucks are either BIPOC- or queer-owned or both, is called **Lil' America**. There's

Above: Portland breakfast—ricotta hotcakes with berries; Below: Take in a game at queer-owned Sports Bra.

Hawker Station for Hainan chicken and rice, **Los Plebes** for Tijuana-style Mexican food, **Frybaby** for Korean fried chicken, **Makulít** for Filipino fast food, a vegan coffee cart called **Speed-o Cappuccino**, and a bunch of others to choose from.

"That whole food-truck pod is also just outside the taproom at **Fracture Brewing**, so you can also get craft beer or cocktails. They host drag shows and yoga and other community events there all the time, too."

NIGHTLIFE SCENE

"Subscribe to the **Queer Social Club** to get on their email list so you know what events are happening when you're visiting. They send out a newsletter every week with upward of 100 upcoming queer events happening in Portland. I'm looking at it right now—one glance and I see a queer salsa night, a Black night market, drag bingo, a comedy show...

"For bars there's **Sports Bra**, which is queer-owned, and their thing is that they only play women's sports. There's also **Crush Bar** here in the southeast, which is a classic gay bar that kind of speaks for itself, but on Friday nights they do host *RuPaul's Drag Race*.

"If you're someone who doesn't drink but you still want to go out and meet people, there's another amazing queer-owned app coming out of Portland called **BuzzCutt**, and they're mapping out all the establishments that have sober options."

GETTING OUTSIDE

"It's such a bike-friendly city. I love to ride the **Waterfront Loop**, a great path along the Willamette River where you can bike and enjoy the views and sounds of the river without leaving the city. As far as parks in the city, **Overlook Park** is a favorite.

"If you have access to a car and time to get out of the city just a touch, there's a clothing-optional beach called **Rooster Rock**. Hundreds of queer people will be there on the weekend if it's nice out.

"And just about 30 minutes outside of the city there's a beach that's also clothing-optional (with clothed sections too) where queer people tend to hang out earlier in the summer: **Sauvie Island**. I'd highly recommend it in the summer, especially. There's berry-picking and a cidery. I'll bike up there—it's about 15 miles [24km] north of here—and hop in the river."

FIRST-TIMER TIPS

"Obviously, I recommend using the Everywhere Is Queer app to find literally hundreds of queer-owned restaurants, shops, bars, and more during your visit. And like I said, I suggest subscribing to the Queer Social Club to get on their list so you know what events are happening when you're visiting. You can totally unsubscribe right after, but you'll have a whole list of queer events going on during your time here.

The More You Know

"Definitely save some room in your suitcase for the vintage shopping; you're going to kick yourself if you don't."

Above: A wealth of wellness at Seagrape Apothecary; *Opposite:* Portland's historic Alphabet District.

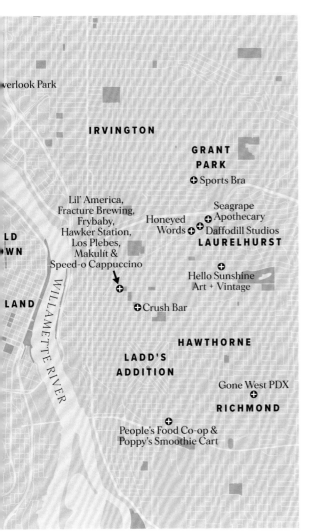

IRVINGTON

GRANT PARK
➕ Sports Bra

verlook Park

Lil' America,
Fracture Brewing,
Frybaby,
Hawker Station,
Los Plebes,
Makulit &
Speed-o Cappuccino

Honeyed
Words ➕➕

Seagrape
➕ Apothecary
➕ Daffodill Studios

LAURELHURST

➕
Hello Sunshine
Art + Vintage

➕ Crush Bar

HAWTHORNE

LADD'S ADDITION

Gone West PDX
➕
RICHMOND

➕
People's Food Co-op &
Poppy's Smoothie Cart

WILLAMETTE RIVER

LD WN

LAND

"Overall, in my experience, I've found Portland to be a very safe city. But that being said, I don't recommend leaving anything in your car, as the most common crime here is that a lot of windows are broken on cars in the city.

"If you like gray and rainy weather, come in the winter. It's not a downpouring rain, it's usually just like a sprinkling rain, so it's definitely still accessible in the winter if you're trying to travel off season. In the summer there's hiking and outdoor culture, beautiful greenery, and parks. Portland is such a beautiful place to visit any time of year, but summer especially.

"Portland's queer community is obviously bonkers. In a good way, of course. So come with an open mind, meet some new people, and enjoy yourself. You're gonna love it."

More Places to Visit

Citizen Ruth

Community Wine Bar

Either/Or

Grindhouse Coffee

Iridescent Daydream

kann

Mutantis Cult Brewery

Roots & Crowns

Puerto Vallarta,

MEXICO

RECOMMENDATIONS BY

Charly Stoever

After traveling to 34 different countries around the world before finally settling down back in their native country—not to be confused with the country they grew up in—nonbinary Latinx money coach, speaker, and Unicorn Millionaire podcast host **Charly Stoever** (they/he) thinks they've finally figured out what led them to fall in love with traveling in the first place.

"I was born in Moravia, Mexico, and moved to the US at three years old, so I was raised undocumented," Charly explained. "For years, I wasn't able to travel at all due to my undocumented status. I think that's what really pushed me to see the world once I was finally able to get the hell out of the US."

Now Charly lives in Puerto Vallarta, a city along the Pacific coast of Mexico, nestled between the lush peaks of the Sierra Madre and the sparkling waters of Banderas Bay.

"You can get your party on, but you can also escape to nature, and that was really important to me," they said of their decision to settle down here. "It's also a very friendly place. I definitely feel safer here as a trans person than I did even in some US states."

Charly typically gauges how queer-friendly a city is on how safe they feel using the bathrooms there—and Puerto Vallarta passes that test with flying colors. "If I use the men's room,

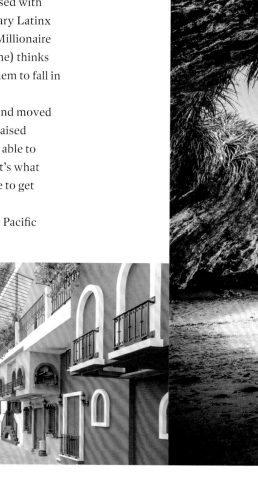

Below: The 'Hidden Beach' of Playa Escondida in the Marietas Islands, offshore of Puerto Vallarta; *Opposite:* A colorful Puerto Vallarta apartment building.

I don't have people yelling at me that I'm using the wrong toilet, like has happened to me other places," they said. "I've had an old man chase me into the bathroom before, and I'm still on guard. I hate public bathrooms. But here, I don't feel like I have to worry about that much."

Charly made a point to mention that as a light-skinned, male-presenting trans person, they feel they have privilege compared to other trans travelers. "That said, Puerto Vallarta is still one of the safest cities not just in Mexico, but in all of Latin America, and it's also a safe space for BIPOC people in general. The people here want to make everyone feel welcome."

AN IDEAL DAY

"I'd get a massage at **Almendras Garden Spa & Beauty**. They're so affordable here, even if you tip really well (which I always do and you should, too), and it's such a relaxing way to start your day.

"Queers love being vegan, queers love being vegetarian. I'm not either of those, but I do love a vegetarian restaurant here called **Planeta Vegetariano**, which is a vegetarian buffet. They have buffet breakfast *and* buffet lunch, and they make their own juices and soy fajitas that actually taste really good.

"Then I would get on a bus headed toward **El Tuito** to go to the **Vallarta Botanical Garden**. I'd spend the rest of the day there, hiking the trails or swimming in **Río Los Horcones**. If I had work to do, I'd bring my laptop with me and do it at the **Hacienda del Oro Restaurant** there, which overlooks the jungle and the gardens.

"I'd probably go for dinner at **Barcelona Tapas Bar**, which is Spanish tapas, not tacos, but I love the view and they have great sangria. I just met a queer traveler there, actually, and from there we ended up going to **La Catrina Cantina**. Once when I went they sang and shared cake with

Above: Our Lady of Guadalupe in Puerto Vallarta's historic center; *Opposite:* When in Mexico...try a pineapple margarita at cocktail hour.

everyone. They have 'Texas Tuesdays' there, too, when a bunch of gay men in cowboy hats and cowboy boots learn how to line dance together, with a crowd of all ages and gender identities."

TOUR THE OUTDOORS

"I did an electric-bike tequila-and-taco tour of the city with my friends through **Los Veranos Canopy Tour** that was a lot of fun. I tried taco stands I'd never seen before that were pretty good. And we went by Elizabeth Taylor's house—Richard Burton and Elizabeth Taylor had their own houses constructed here when he was here to film *The Night of the Iguana*. Now that house is a restaurant called the **Iguana**.

"Definitely do a snorkeling tour at **Los Arcos**. Whale-watching season, December to March, is also really cool there. Sometimes I'll just sit at the beach and look up and see humpback whales breaching.

"There's a beach here called **Playa Los Muertos**, and that's where the fit guys go to cruise and walk around in their Speedos. There's also a beach south of town called **Conchas Chinas** (Spanish for 'Chinese shells') that you can walk to. The water is clean and clear and turquoise, and you can see pelicans diving right in the water."

FINDING QUEER COMMUNITY

"I would start by going to **Elixir Mixology Bar**. It's the only lesbian-owned bar here. The queer scene here is small, so everybody kind of knows everybody. You can ask the bartenders or the owners at Elixir what queer events are going on while you're here, and if they can add you to the local queer WhatsApp groups.

"There's a Black-owned restaurant here called **Brooklyn Cafe**, where a lot of the queer people in those WhatsApp groups meet up for brunch. There's also a cafe called **Chakrana**, where you can buy psilocybin-mushroom capsules. They make smoothies that they infuse with it, too, and chocolates.

"Every Wednesday there's an art walk in **El Centro Histórico** from 6pm to 10pm, where all the (mostly gay) art-gallery owners open up their doors. People dress up for that, by which I mean they wear their nice Hawaiian shirts and their nice khaki shorts. They might even cover a toe or two, we don't know.

"There's a **night market** at the **Marina Vallarta Malecón** (the boardwalk) every Thursday from 6pm to 10pm, where something like 200 different vendors set up stalls to sell food and clothes but also crafts and crystals. It's great for people-watching and it's right there on the **Marina Vallarta Malecón**. There is also a ballroom

The More You Know

"Don't drink the tap water. Always buy bottled water. And bring hand sanitizer everywhere you go."

Above: Los Arcos National Marine Park, just south of Puerto Vallarta; **Opposite:** Pescado zarandeado— grilled fish, Mexican-style.

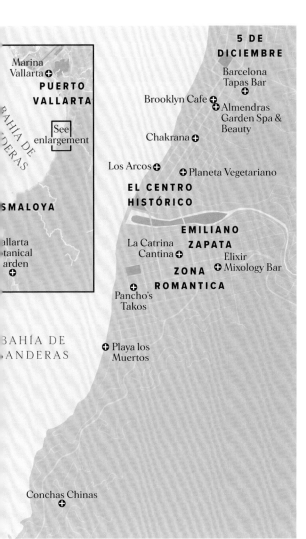

5 DE DICIEMBRE

Marina Vallarta ⊕

PUERTO VALLARTA

Barcelona Tapas Bar ⊕

Brooklyn Cafe ⊕

⊕ Almendras Garden Spa & Beauty

See enlargement

Chakrana ⊕

Los Arcos ⊕ ⊕ Planeta Vegetariano

EL CENTRO HISTÓRICO

EMILIANO ZAPATA

La Catrina Cantina ⊕

Elixir ⊕ Mixology Bar

ZONA ROMANTICA

⊕ Pancho's Takos

BAHÍA DE BANDERAS

⊕ Playa los Muertos

Conchas Chinas ⊕

scene here. **Kiki House of Paradise** hosts amazing ballroom performances and competitions that put local trans and gender nonconforming hotties in the spotlight."

FIRST-TIMER TIPS

"Buses in between cities are nicer, not the buses that stay within the city. A few have air conditioning because they're new, but some of the older ones can get really hot.

"Always Uber, never a taxi. If they hear your accent and that you're not from Puerto Vallarta, you might be charged the 'foreigner tax.'

"If a taco stand has a lot of people, that's a good sign. If a taco stand has nobody waiting in line, I'd be cautious. The bigger the line, the more poppin' the place. There's a place called **Pancho's Takos** that will even give you a margarita while you wait in line. If you prefer to avoid the big crowds, **Tacos El Moreno** is a great locally run stand in the **Zona Romantica**.

"Most importantly, just come with an open mind. There's always something going on here. If you feel lonely, just connect. There's nothing wrong with saying to someone here, 'Hey, I'm on my own and I'm trying to make friends while I'm here, is there anything going on?' A lot of people do speak English here, and they'll answer you in English because they want you to feel welcome."

Above: *Waterside views of Richmond's concrete-arched railway bridge over the James River.*

Richmond,
USA

RECOMMENDATIONS BY

Paige Poprocky

KNOW BEFORE YOU GO

LANGUAGE
English

CURRENCY
USD ($)

PRIDE CELEBRATIONS
Annually in September

WHEN TO GO
During shoulder season (March–June or September–November) for the best weather: sunny and temperate, but not excessively hot or humid

While she's not technically a born-and-raised Richmonder, after she moved from Pennsylvania to Virginia in 2012, **Paige Poprocky** (she/her) *did* experience a period of what she'd consider rebirth.

At the time, Paige was working as a teacher, married to a man who worked as a police officer. "We met when I was 16, and we started dating when I was 18. It was just easy. Then we moved in together and got married and it was like, 'OK, I guess this is what I do next,'" she said. "But he and I both knew I was attracted to women, and he was fine with it. He agreed to let me experiment a little over the years, so I did, and that was fine for a while."

But over time, it wasn't enough. "I hated my job, I hated my house, I hated living in the suburbs. I just hated it all so much. And all of that hate made me numb. I was just numb to everything," Paige recalled. Her only solace at the time was the wine blog she'd started in 2019, Sips and Trips with Paige—but eventually, that alone wasn't enough, either.

Finally, she reached her boiling point. "I told my husband that things weren't working anymore. We parted ways, and that had this sort of domino effect: I quit my job, I moved out on my own into an apartment in the city, and I got a full-time job working in social media at

The Richmond Experience," Paige said. She also met her girlfriend, Holly, who was going through her own divorce with her now ex-wife. The two started dating, and three years later, they bought a condo in the **Scott's Addition** neighborhood and moved in together.

Paige credits the city of Richmond for inspiring her to step into her authentic identity. "When I came to Richmond, it opened up my eyes to the world," Paige said. "I saw people like me here—people who were visibly queer—and it made me feel like I didn't have to hide that part of me anymore. I could be myself. I could finally feel again. Eventually, it hit me: 'Oh, *this* is what happiness feels like.'"

QUEER EVERYWHERE

"I feel like queerness has always been in Richmond's DNA. Richmond is so vibrant, very artsy, and diverse. Frankly, it's weird here. It's weird! And we like it that way. That's what makes it so quirky and fun, and I think that's part of what makes it so queer-friendly, too.

"I know in the past, the gayborhood might have been in **The Fan** [district] or over near **VCU [Virginia Commonwealth University]**, but now it's so much more spread out. I think that's just because of how progressive Richmond has become over the years. Now, it's just kind of queer-friendly everywhere around the city instead of just in one spot.

"In my experience, I feel comfortable to be myself everywhere in Richmond. I can be out with Holly, holding hands, being lovey-dovey, and it's all good."

SCOTT'S ADDITION

"Ten years ago, the **Scott's Addition** neighborhood used to be a lot of industrial buildings and warehouses. Now it's what we call Richmond's 'beverage district' because it's home to more than a dozen craft breweries, cideries, distilleries, and even a meadery. If you're looking for the best spot to do a beer crawl or to go barhopping, this is it. But the neighborhood also has so many restaurants, coffee shops, arcades and game bars, a bowling alley... It's a really unique place.

"A few of our favorite places in the area are **Väsen Brewing Company** for the beer, the **Hof (Hofheimer)** just because we love the rooftop, and **Starr Hill Beer Hall & Rooftop** for beer *and* a rooftop. I also love **Brambly Park**, which is an urban winery with a huge outdoor area. They have a lot of live music and a huge park area, so it's dog-friendly and kid-friendly."

AN IDEAL DAY

"Start your day right with drag brunch at **Godfrey's**. From there, there's a lot of fun to be had in nearby **Carytown**—you could spend a whole day there. Catch a movie at the **Byrd Theater**. Check out cool queer-owned shops like **Mongrel**. Get lunch at one of the dozens of restaurants along the strip like **Galaxy Diner**. Go to the **Jasper** for drinks. Have a French dinner at **Can Can Brasserie**. And, of course, you have to go dancing at **Babes [of Carytown]**. It was founded in the '70s as Richmond's original lesbian bar, but now it's open to anyone in the queer community. Or, if you're not into dancing, you can just go outside and play on their beach volleyball courts."

Above: Portland's skyline from the T Tyler Potterfield Memorial Bridge; Below: Forest Hill Park in fall.

WINING & DINING

"For something upscale: **L'Opossum**. The queer chef and owner there was a nominee for a James Beard Award, and the food is to die for. Make a reservation, though. I'd also recommend **Lost Letter**, which is a rustic Italian restaurant with a great wine list. **Grisette** is another great restaurant in **Church Hill**. Their steak frites! And wine. Across the street from there is **Alewife**, if you want amazing seafood. Their sister restaurant, **Odyssey**, is also a favorite—their escargot!

"For a more casual dinner, go to **Joe's Inn**. It's a Richmond institution. Eat all the pasta; you won't regret it. **LUNCH. SUPPER!** is a great casual option, too; Holly and I go there all the time. And we always go to **Sabai** for Thai food and tropical cocktails. That's probably our number-one takeout spot."

GETTING OUTSIDE

"Here's my favorite loop downtown: I park near the **Virginia War Memorial**, then I go to **Brown's Island** to walk around there first. From there, I cross over the **T Tyler Potterfield Memorial Bridge**; locals call it the 'T Pott' or 'teapot' bridge. You get a gorgeous view of the city when you're out there over the **James River**.

The More You Know

"My best advice is to stay in the city and immerse yourself in whatever is going on while you're here. Pick a neighborhood—The Fan, Scott's Addition, Church Hill, wherever—and just wander. It's a safe, interesting city, and there's always something going on."

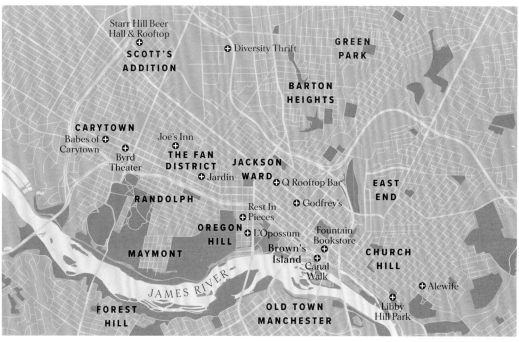

Then I head toward the **Flood Wall**, which is a cool feature in Richmond, before I cross over to the **Mayo Bridge**, which connects to the **Richmond Slave Trail**. We have a lot of history here, which you can read on placards along that trail in particular. Then that takes us to the **Canal Walk**, where you can usually see people on our **Riverfront Canal Cruises**, which are really nice for visitors, too—you get to learn a lot about the city's history. Then it's a short walk back to where we started on **Brown's Island**. The whole loop is about 3 miles [5km], and it's easily one of our favorite things to do in Richmond."

PARKS, MARKETS & PATIOS

"**Maymont** [**Park**] is massive and so underrated. Holly and I go there all the time and just sprawl out on a picnic blanket in the sunshine. Another great spot for a picnic is **Libby Hill Park** in **Church Hill**, where you get a stunning view of the Richmond skyline and the James River. And we have **Scuffletown Park**, this little pocket park, that's one of Richmond's sweetest hidden gems.

Below: Pick up something unique at Richmond's Diversity Thrift; Opposite: Craft-beer heaven at Väsen Brewing Company, Scott's Addition.

"We also have some awesome farmers markets here on the weekends. On Saturdays, we have **RVA Big Market**, which is in **Bryan Park** in the **Lakeside** neighborhood. There are all kinds of cool things to do in that area—**Lewis Ginter Botanical Garden** is a local favorite. Then every Sunday, there's the **South of the James Market** in **Forest Hill**. That puts you right near **Forest Hill Park**. The **Forest Hill Park Trail** is about 3 miles [5km] as well, and it's a part of the larger **James River Park System**, which is made up of something like 22 miles [35km] of trails, ranging from beginner to advanced.

"My favorite place with a patio is probably **Jardin**, a wine bar in the Fan. It's like our *Cheers* bar. Richmond also has a bunch of rooftop bars, like **Q Rooftop Bar** and the **Byrd House** in the **Arts District**, **Havana '59** in **Shockoe Bottom**, and **Harry's at Hofheimer** in Scott's Addition. People flock there when it's nice outside."

UNIQUELY RICHMOND

"**Oregon Hill** is a fun, creepy spot. You can walk through the **Hollywood Cemetery**, which is beautiful any time of year, but especially when the trees are in bloom or in autumn when the leaves start to fall. And really close to there is this shop called **Rest in Pieces**, where you can find things like crystals, books about witchcraft, taxidermy animals: 'oddities and curiosities.'

"For shopping, especially if you're a queer traveler, **Diversity Thrift** and **Ashby** are two really cool secondhand shops that are especially loved by Richmond's queer community. There's a shop called **Odd Bird** in **Jackson Ward** that carries a lot of funky stuff that's fun to look through, too. For books, **Fountain Bookstore** and **Shelf Life** are two local favorites, and **bbgb** is a children's bookstore that often hosts drag-queen reading hours for children. **Small Friend Records & Books** is another great one—a queer, woman-owned radical bookstore that also sells records."

FIRST-TIMER TIPS

"Richmond is a real festival city. Each May we have **Riverrock**, which is an outdoor sports and music festival, as well as the **Lebanese Food Festival** and the **Richmond Greek Festival**. Every June, we also host our **Friday Cheers** live concert series every weekend on Brown's Island. In July, we've got the **Shakespeare Festival** and **Festival of the Arts**. In August, it's the **Watermelon Festival**. Each September, we host **Richmond PrideFest**, along with the **Richmond Folk Festival**. There are just always events happening.

"We have so many touristy things to do here, and I recommend just embracing them. Even the people who live here get into the touristy things! If you're looking to take a tour of Richmond, I love **RVATukTuk**. **Discover Richmond Tours** are great, too—they're food tours and beverage tours led by super-friendly locals. **RVA Brew Crew** is another good one, especially if you're traveling with a group that might want to do a brewery hop or barhop, so you can get safely from A to B without someone having to volunteer to be the designated driver."

Opposite: Take in the world-class collection at Richmond's Virginia Museum of Fine Arts.

Saugatuck & Douglas,
USA

RECOMMENDATIONS BY

Daniel DeFranco

Growing up just outside of New York City, **Daniel DeFranco** (he/him) never had any interest in small-town life. So, when his grad-school boyfriend—now husband—invited him to spend a weekend at a friend's cabin in Saugatuck, Michigan, his expectations were admittedly low.

"I had never even heard of it," Daniel remembered. "But we got there and it just blew me away."

Picture a walkable community, colorful neighborhood characters, architecture frozen in time in the early 20th century, and not a chain store or modern apartment complex in sight. Now make it a little gayer—add one of the largest LGBTQIA+ resorts in the country, the **Dunes Resort**, and a litany of queer artists studying at nearby **Ox-Bow School of Art**—and you've got a pretty good mental picture of Saugatuck.

Daniel and his husband were enamored. They began returning to Saugatuck as frequently as they could. "We were coming up so often that we started to realize, 'Maybe this isn't just a vacation destination for us.' There are a lot of people who weren't born here but decided to move here later

Below: Lakeside lounging in Saugatuck; **Opposite:** *Apple Fest at Virtue Cider, just outside of Saugatuck-Douglas.*

in life because of how they felt when they visited. They made the conscious decision, 'This feels like home, and I want to be here full-time,' and so did we."

Eight years later, Daniel has graduated to 'local' status in Saugatuck, a badge of honor second only to the 'native' medal worn by the select few who were born and raised within the township's borders.

He's not alone, of course. Many LGBTQ+ visitors have come to Saugatuck and sister-city Douglas for a good time, exploring the work of local artists and partying at the Dunes until the wee hours of the morning, only to decide that they want to extend their stay or make their time there permanent.

"There's a real sense of community. There are people here from all walks of life. The diversity is part of the quality of life here. And we're all together and everyone's welcome and included everywhere," Daniel said. "It changed my perception about small-town life, that it could have this strong sense of community and of pride. Here, my experience as someone who is gay is actually something that's being valued, as opposed to being a reason not to fit in."

SEEING SAUGATUCK

"**Butler St** is kind of like the heart of town. There are little offshoot-like streets with restaurants and bars. And it's not like, 'this is a gay-friendly spot, that's a straight spot.' Everybody hangs out everywhere.

"My favorite restaurant in that area is **Phil's Bar & Grille**. Their food is the best in town, elevated without being froufrou. The staff is warm and kind, and I think that's one of the reasons that if you do sit down at Phil's bar, you're going to feel welcome right away. So, I recommend sitting at the bar if you want to meet a lot of people.

"If you want to go a little fancier, there's a restaurant called **Bowdie's Chophouse**, but make reservations in the summertime.

"Restaurants probably stop serving food around 9pm or 10pm on weeknights, maybe 10pm or 11pm on weekends, but there are places you can still go to drink and socialize after those hours for more of a 'late-night' vibe.

"For drinks a bit later in the evening you could go to **Wicks Park Bar & Grille** on Water St. **Wally's Bar & Grill** is another bar with an eclectic crowd, just off of Water St.

"We have a piano bar right on the water called the **Annex**, and there's even a stage up on top of the piano. Then there's **Corner Bar & Grill**, where they do karaoke every Friday and Saturday.

"If I were a younger traveler, queer, maybe single, I'd check out the **Sand Bar Saloon**. It's our quintessential dive bar. They usually have a jazz band playing, an old-school jazz band off in the corner."

DOWNTOWN DOUGLAS

"Douglas is a whole different vibe than downtown Saugatuck. It's a little more laid-back, not as busy. So, if you want to escape the Saugatuck craziness, I would definitely recommend visiting downtown Douglas. They do have restaurants and art galleries there.

"There's a restaurant in Douglas called **Everyday People Cafe** and a newer restaurant called **Wild Dog**, if you want a nicer meal, and they do have a really nice bar, too.

"There's a bar in downtown Douglas called **Borrowed Time**, and in their basement there's an old speakeasy that was a gay bar with a long history. Since the township was founded in the 1820s to 1830s, that speakeasy has always been a safe space for people in the LGBTQ+ community, which not only brought a lot of 'transplants' to move here but made future generations comfortable to be totally themselves and to be accepting of others outside of just the bars and speakeasies."

THE DUNES

"As the story goes, the owners—the couple that started the **Dunes**, Carl and Larry—were both bartenders at a bar in downtown Saugatuck called the Blue Tempo. It was a jazz bar, and it was really the first gay bar to open in Saugatuck. It burned down in the late '60s or early '70s, and then Carl and Larry decided to buy what I believe was a Howard Johnson hotel [US former hotel chain] at the time. They started renovating it, and it would become what's now

Above: Lake Michigan fall color along the Saugatuck shoreline;
Opposite: *Alfresco drinks at Virtue Cider in nearby Fennville.*

The More You Know

"Everything is local, no chains. You're not going to find a CVS or a Walgreens [two US pharmacy store chains]. We have a downtown pharmacy and drugstore, but you're not going to find specialty stuff there."

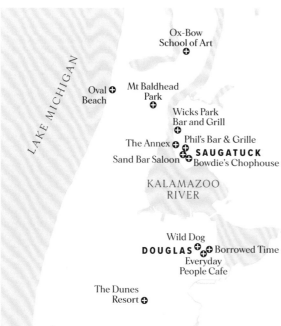

LAKE MICHIGAN

Ox-Bow School of Art

Oval Beach

Mt Baldhead Park

Wicks Park Bar and Grill

The Annex

Phil's Bar & Grille

SAUGATUCK

Sand Bar Saloon

Bowdie's Chophouse

KALAMAZOO RIVER

Wild Dog

DOUGLAS

Borrowed Time

Everyday People Cafe

The Dunes Resort

LAKE MICHIGAN

Saugatuck Dunes State Park

See enlargement

SAUGATUCK

DOUGLAS

Virtue Cider

Modales Wines

the Dunes today, our area's famous gay resort and a real haven for gay travelers.

"Over the years, the new owners have really invested in it. They built out this gorgeous pool with cabana areas. Inside, there's a cabaret and a dance floor. Then there's an even bigger dance floor outside, too. And if you go there in the summer for Memorial Day, July Fourth, or Labor Day, there are people all over the dance floor, and it is such a blast."

GETTING OUTSIDE

"**Oval Beach** is a lot of fun. I would recommend the **Saugatuck Dunes**, about five minutes outside of town. It's a state park covering over 1000 acres [405 hectares], all woods and sand dunes. The beach is huge and gorgeous.

"There's also what we call Mt Baldy, or **Mt Baldhead**. It's a huge sand dune, over 230ft [70m] high, with this massive staircase with views from the top. And there are all great hiking

*Below: On the deck at the Borrowed Time bar in Douglas; **Opposite:** Partying at the lakeside Dunes Resort.*

trails in that area. A trail called the **Crow's Nest** takes you to a peninsula in the **Tallmadge Woods** where you can see the original mouth of the **Kalamazoo River**, with hundreds of acres of preserved land.

"We're part of the Great Lakes region, of course, so **Lake Michigan** really dominates our identity. There are 100ft [30m] dunes and huge forests, and we're right on the lake that's so huge it looks like it could be the ocean.

"It feels kind of East Coast, because we're surrounded by water and there are boats everywhere. And it's a little bit like a throwback when you first see it. You're like, 'OK, this looks like it's from the 1950s.' But that's one of the best parts of life here—we're a little bit shielded from the pressures of the outside world."

DAY TRIPS

"There's a local art school you can visit called **Ox-Bow**, and every other Friday night they do an open house where you can try demos in metalworking, glassblowing, multimedia painting, all sorts of things. They usually have drinks, and then they have an option to see some of the art pieces students have made. It's a unique experience that a lot of locals like to do. You park at the Mt Baldy parking lot and then the shuttle runs you right to Ox-Bow, so that's a great way to experience the local arts scene.

"We have a winery worth visiting, too: **Modales Wines**, and they've done just a fabulous job. The winery is set within the vineyards on this huge farm and has a big outdoor tasting room, so you really get the whole experience. Fridays and Saturdays they usually have live music and food trucks. It's a winemaker out of California, so you're not gonna get some, like, strawberry wine or whatever; it's gonna be nice. They have a great dry Riesling.

"And then we have **Virtue Cider**, which was started by Greg Hall. He used to be the brewmaster at Goose Island Brewery in Chicago, but he sold Goose Island to Anheuser-Busch for a decent chunk of change, then he moved the operation to **Fennville** just outside of Saugatuck-Douglas. He built these French, Normandy-style farmhouses, and started making all of these small-batch ciders aged in French barrels. You can walk around and they have some farm animals. It's supposed to be kind of like a small French farm. It's really cool.

"For budget travelers looking for an immersive social experience, absolutely check out **Camp-It**, a spacious property just outside of town with great amenities and activities for the LGBTQ+ traveler. If you're looking for a romantic experience or a peaceful place to reconnect with friends, the **Lakeshore Resort** is a gorgeous spot located right on Lake Michigan."

FIRST-TIMER TIPS

"We're very casual. And that can be interpreted any way you like; it just doesn't mean formal. You can truly wear whatever you want, and it's always fun to see all of the different fashion choices. It's a colorful community.

"Don't be afraid to engage with other people. Everyone is typically here to have a good time, even the locals.

"It's an inspiring place, so come experience it yourself. You've never seen anything quite like Saugatuck-Douglas."

Opposite: Cute-as-a-button Kalamazoo Replica Lighthouse, on the Lake Michigan shore in Douglas.

Above: *Sunset serenity at Vancouver's Stanley Park.*

Vancouver,
CANADA

RECOMMENDATIONS BY
Barb Snelgrove

KNOW BEFORE YOU GO

LANGUAGE
English

CURRENCY
Canadian
Dollar ($)

PRIDE CELEBRATIONS
Annually at the
end of July/
beginning
of August

WHEN TO GO
March–
November for
mild weather,
December–
February for
winter sports

As a proud born-and-raised, second-generation Vancouverite, **Barb Snelgrove** (she/her) hasn't ever really considered moving away from her hometown.

"I could never stray far, it is too beautiful," Barb said. "To live in a city that has all the amenities of an urban lifestyle and yet be able to head to a park or beach—and within minutes be immediately immersed in true natural surroundings that immediately strip away the tensions of a concrete jungle—is a blessing I will never grow tired of."

Situated on the West Coast of Canada in British Columbia, on the sovereign, unceded land of the **xʷməθkʷəy̓əm** (Musqueam), **Skwxwú7mesh** (Squamish), and **səl̓ílwəta?ɬ** (Tsleil-Waututh) Peoples, Vancouver has long been a safe haven for queer travelers.

Like much of North America's West Coast, it's known as a relaxed city. "We definitely work to live, not live to work," Barb said. "We are well known for our laid-back style, boundless outdoor recreation options, and stunning natural beauty wherever you look."

One of the first aspects of Vancouver's natural beauty that you might notice? "The palm trees," Barb said. "That alone should tell you that Vancouver's climate is more hospitable than what people usually associate with a trip to Canada."

As the producer and host of Canada's longest-running queer radio show **QueerFM Van** and a 2013 inductee of the **Canadian Q Hall of Fame**, Barb—better known locally as **@megamouthmedia**—was more than happy to share her go-to recommendations for queer travelers in LGBTQ+-friendly Vancouver.

"There is always plenty to see and do for **2SLGBTQIA+** travelers to Vancouver, no matter what time of the year you travel here," she said, the '2S' at the start of the acronym here referring to the 'two-spirit,' a person who identifies as having both a masculine and a feminine spirit, and is used by some Indigenous people to describe their sexual, gender and/or spiritual identity. "Our mild climate keeps us busy with a vibrant queer culture that buzzes year-round."

GAYBORHOODS

"There are two distinct communities where LGBTQIA+ folk can really soak up the local queer vibe. In the heart of downtown Vancouver's **West End** we have the historically queer **Davie Village**, and on the **East Side** of Vancouver, the **Commercial Drive** district has a cool boho, artsy feel. "If you want to put your pink dollars to work, **Womyn's Ware** is located in this lesbian and gender-nonconforming area of **Commercial Drive**. It's the top sex-positive adult store in town and has friendly, knowledgeable staff. They also have a small business incorporated into the store called **Your Open Closet**, offering undergarments for trans people.

"Also on the East Side, in a half-circle block off of **Fraser St**, is **Burcu's Angels**. The owner is a longtime ally of the queer community and a local legend in Vancouver fashion circles, and the beautifully curated selection of secondhand and vintage clothing is the best in the city.

"Davie Village is home to the **Little Sister's Book & Art Emporium**, the community gathering spot for all things queer in Vancouver. It's the gayest shop in the 'Village'; you know you've found home from the minute you walk into the store and see the racks of rainbow-themed offerings. This bookstore is famous for having taken the federal government of Canada's Customs Agency to court for censorship and holding up queer book shipments at the border. After years of court battles, they finally won, and their store still proudly stands as a beacon for 2SLGBTQIA+ rights.

"The neighborhood is known for its **Rainbow Crosswalk** next to **Jim Deva Plaza**. While in the village, I recommend taking the **Really Gay History Tour**, put on by local tour company **Forbidden Vancouver Walking Tours**, highlighting the queer history of Vancouver.

"Just a quick 10-minute walk down the hill to **Denman St**, you can find plenty of photo ops at the **A-maze-ing Laughter Statues** at **Morton Park** across from **English Bay Beach**.

"If time permits, visit the **SUM Gallery** at the **Sun Wah Centre** in the **Chinatown** district, one of the only permanent galleries worldwide dedicated to the presentation of queer art."

GETTING OUTSIDE

"It wouldn't be a visit to Vancouver without a trip to **Stanley Park**, with over 400 hectares [990 acres] of natural West Coast rainforest. Vancouver also has many miles of gorgeous beaches, including **Locarno** and **Jericho Beaches**, **Spanish Banks**, and **Acadia Beach**. These shorelines are a favorite playground for locals. Paddleboarders, paragliders, kayakers, and swimmers all share space with sunseekers, volleyball players, and local wildlife. There are regular sightings of bald eagles, seals, otters, and orca whales, so have your camera ready!

Above: Steeping out over the Davie Village Rainbow Crosswalk on Vancouver's Really Gay History Tour; *Below:* Among old-growth forest on the Capilano Suspension Bridge.

"Just a few minutes further west of this strip of beaches is **Wreck Beach**, voted one of the most beautiful nude beaches in the world. It also hosts a 'gay beach' section, where a predominantly male gay populace can be found sunning in their birthday suits and enjoying the...'views' throughout the warmer months. **Trail 6** will get you to Wreck Beach, but follow signs to **Trail 7** for the queer element.

"Vancouver is also home to the world's longest uninterrupted waterfront path, the **Seawall**, at more than 28km [17 miles]. It's divided into two sections: one for walkers and joggers, and one for cyclists and in-line skaters.

"I recommend a trip up to the **Gondola at Grouse Mountain [Skyride]** for a breathtaking view of the city and seascape. To get to North Vancouver where it's located—or as locals call it, the **North Shore**—you can take the **Lions Gate Bridge** for the experience alone.

"Close by to Grouse Mountain in North Vancouver is the **Capilano Suspension Bridge**, where you can immerse yourself in some of British Columbia's spectacular old-growth forests. But be warned: if you have a fear of heights, this might not be for you.

The More You Know

"If you plan to visit
Vancouver in the
summer, don't miss
Western Canada's
largest Pride Parade,
where hundreds
of thousands of
queers and allies
flock to Downtown
Vancouver for a week
of celebration, cultural
events, street parties,
festivals and concerts
that culminate with
the Vancouver Pride
Parade and Festival."

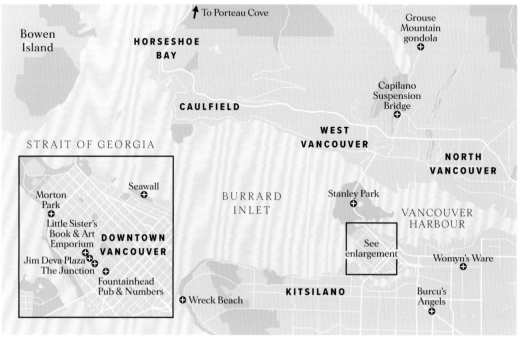

↑ To Porteau Cove

Bowen
Island

**HORSESHOE
BAY**

Grouse
Mountain
gondola ⊕

Capilano
Suspension
Bridge ⊕

CAULFIELD

**WEST
VANCOUVER**

**NORTH
VANCOUVER**

STRAIT OF GEORGIA

Seawall ⊕

Morton
Park ⊕

Little Sister's
Book & Art
Emporium ⊕

Jim Deva Plaza ⊕⊕
The Junction ⊕

**DOWNTOWN
VANCOUVER**

Fountainhead
Pub & Numbers

BURRARD
INLET

Stanley Park
⊕

VANCOUVER
HARBOUR

See
enlargement

Womyn's Ware
⊕

KITSILANO

⊕ Wreck Beach

Burcu's
Angels
⊕

"There are three ski hills located within a half-hour of the city center (**Cypress**, **Grouse**, and **Seymour Mountains**) offering world-class ski runs. During the summer months, these same mountains offer plenty of great hiking and biking options. A must-do for any outdoors person is the **Grouse Grind**, a 2.9km [1.8-mile] trail up the face of Grouse Mountain, commonly referred to as 'Mother Nature's StairMaster.' Grouse even offers an app where you can monitor your performance and see how you rank against other 'Grinders' from around the world."

GETTING AROUND

"Buses, taxis, Ubers, ferries and rideshare bike-rental stations are situated all over town, so everything is easily accessible.

"There are two companies that zip back and forth to get folks from the downtown core to the West Side of the water. Run by **False Creek Ferries** and the rainbow-colored **Aquabus**, these cute forms of transit give you literally a water-level marine view of Vancouver's shoreline."

*Below: Spot harbor seals from Vancouver's shoreline; **Opposite:** Flying the rainbow flag at Vancouver Pride Parade and Festival.*

NIGHTLIFE & CELEBRATIONS

"The queer scene in Davie Village has bars like the **Junction**, **Fountainhead Pub**, **Pumpjack Pub**, **1181**, **Numbers**, and **Celebrities Nightclub**, which all stay open to 2am in the morning, and sometimes those hours are extended on holiday long weekends.

"Vancouver's drag community has long been recognized for their considerable talents. You could easily 'Rent a Queen' and have a pop-up party at a local restaurant—trust me when I tell you that this is *not* uncommon."

DAY TRIPS

"A trip to **Bowen Island**, a small island municipality that is part of Metro Vancouver, is a short ferry ride from **Horseshoe Bay**, just past West Vancouver. You can putter around the village visiting the local artisan shops, enjoy fresh goods from the bakery, and chill at one of the many patios or parks.

"Aside from that, 45 minutes out of town and found along the Sea-to-Sky Highway is the **Sea to Sky Gondola**, between Vancouver and Whistler. The views from the top of the mountain are jaw-dropping.

"Along the Sea-to-Sky corridor, there are also some great areas for scuba diving, including **Porteau Cove** and **Whytecliff Park**. Most people equate tropical locales with scuba diving, but Vancouver maintains a reputation for some of the best cold-water scuba diving in the world."

Melbourne,
AUSTRALIA

RECOMMENDATIONS BY

Aurelia St Clair

Like many Melburnians, **Aurelia St Clair** (she/her) may have moved to Melbourne for an ex, but when things didn't work out, she—like many Melburnians—stayed for the vibes.

"Melbourne has a really queer vibe, because I think a lot of people in small towns grow up and move here to come out," Aurelia said. "We have a vibrant arts community, gay marriage is legal here, and overall I feel really safe here."

In the decade since she arrived in Melbourne, writer and comedian Aurelia has made quite the name for herself in the Victorian capital city, performing at the **Melbourne International Comedy Festival** four out of the 10 years she's lived there and cohosting the award-winning pop culture podcast, **POPGAYS**, to critical acclaim.

Aurelia also met the woman who would become her wife, and settled down in the west of Melbourne, particularly for the area's artistic vibes. "I think people often compare Australia and the US: Melbourne is like New York and Sydney is more like LA," she explained. "Melbourne is a bit more grungy. People wear a lot of black, and the weather in the winter gets quite cold. It's not the Australian vibe of sun and surfing and being at the beach all the time that Sydney has."

That said, Aurelia was quick to mention that both cities have a thriving LGBTQ+ population

*Below: Dusk over Federation Square, on the fringes of the CBD; **Opposite:** A memorable meal in Melbourne.*

KNOW BEFORE YOU GO
....

LANGUAGE
English

CURRENCY
Australian Dollar ($)

PRIDE CELEBRATIONS
Midsumma Festival, annually in late January through early February

WHEN TO GO
Australian summer (October–March, with peak summer in December and January)

and plenty for visitors to see and do. "Ideally, I think you'd want to do a road trip. That's a really common way to explore Australia and something I did when I first arrived as well," she said. "You can drive straight from Melbourne to Sydney, but it's nicest when you take the long way along the coast and stop in a few towns along the way."

"But if you're pressed for time, the flight between Sydney and Melbourne is only about an hour and a half long," Aurelia added, though a road trip with a pit stop at the **Big Murray Cod** in **Tocumwal** admittedly does sound like more fun.

AN IDEAL DAY

"Stay in the center of the city, which we call the **CBD**. From the CBD you could easily walk pretty much anywhere you want to go, or you could take the trams, which are quite intuitive to use.

"There's a really rich history of immigration in Australia, from Italian, Greek, and other European immigrants coming after WWII and setting up coffee bars, so there's a lot of good coffee in Melbourne. There's great cuisine from all corners of the world but the coffee culture here is particularly influenced by Europe, and you'll find a lot of small businesses and people that are obsessed with their local coffee spot. My local is called **Migrant Coffee**. It's run by a group of women that are POC and queer as well, so I love it there, supporting my own community.

"For brunch or breakfast, try [the suburbs/neighborhoods of] **Fitzroy** or **Collingwood**. Or if you want to have a very Melbourne experience, you can line up to have something that does taste good but is also super overhyped on social media, like a croissant from **Lune** bakery. From there, you could walk to the **Fitzroy Market**, which is every weekend, for food and vintage clothes.

Above: Head to Melbourne's Fitzroy district for dining, drinks or shopping at stores like Books for Cooks;
***Opposite:** Escape the city to forest-bathe in the nearby Yarra Ranges.*

"While Australia's famous for beaches, you'd have to leave Melbourne to go to a really nice one. So, if you wanted to spend the day in the city, I would go to **Fitzroy Pool** instead, which is walking distance from the market, and it's a busy spot for younger locals to sunbathe. It's definitely a very queer spot to spend your day."

GAYBORHOOD

"There's **Smith St** in Fitzroy, which has a few gay clubs and pubs. **Yah Yahs** has a lip-sync competition on Thursdays; that's definitely geared toward your younger queer crowd. And then on the same street there's a place called **Sircuit**, which is more gay than queer really, with more of a club vibe. They have drag nights as well, and a restaurant where you can sit down and watch drag shows while you have dinner with your friends.

"On the same street is the **86** bar. It's also a queer spot for club nights and drag performances, but during the week you can also just go to have a drink and it's a bit more chill. In that same area on **Peel St** is a gay pub called the **Peel**, and it's definitely a bit more gay than lesbian. But recently, a new lesbian bar opened in the same suburb called **Beans Bar**."

GETTING OUTDOORS

"For an outdoorsy day, I would do something like the **1000 Steps Walk (Kokoda Track Memorial Walk)**, about 45 minutes outside of Melbourne. It's not actually 1000 steps, but it definitely feels like it. It's a nice way to see some of the local bush area. There are beautiful redwood forests about an hour outside of Melbourne as well, in the **Yarra Ranges**, which are worth a visit.

"Then just about an hour and a half away from Melbourne, still in **Victoria**, are beautiful hot springs. The **Peninsula Hot Springs** has about 20 different pools, and there's a beautiful outlook while you're soaking in a hot tub.

"Or if you want to go to a spa closer to Melbourne, **Sense of Self** is a bathhouse with a steam room, a sauna, a cold plunge, mineral bath... The vibe is very serene."

ARTS & CULTURE

"There's the **National Gallery of Victoria**, which is one of the largest art galleries not only in the country but in the world. They have some gorgeous pieces and they host events like a queer youth charity ball, which I've had the chance to emcee before. They always have a kids' exhibit that accompanies whatever major exhibit they have at the moment. There's a cafe and a restaurant attached to the National, and it's within walking distance of the center of the city. Or you can check out **ACMI**, which is a moving-pictures type of gallery, with films and animations that are suitable for all ages.

"You can also find musical theater and theater performances at the **Arts Centre**. In the summer, there's also an open-air theater called **Sidney Myer Music Bowl**, with great programming and international acts. You'll see people setting up picnic blankets to see artists perform. We saw Nile Rodgers and Chaka Khan there. If you like live music in smaller settings, there's also a suburb called **St Kilda** with an iconic venue called the 'Espy,' or the **Esplanade Hotel**.

"And around the corner in **St Kilda** is the **Victorian Pride Centre**, which is a massive, beautiful, government-supported space. It has a queer bookshop inside and queer markets on certain days. Their programming includes drag, comedy, theater, and more."

The More You Know

"The weather can be a bit unpredictable in spring and autumn— it'll start off really sunny, then all of a sudden start hailing. So, pack an umbrella or maybe just buy one when you get here. And bring something with sleeves, even if it's summer, because you never know."

Above: *Ready to take your order at a CBD bar;* **Opposite:** *Shopping in Melbourne Central.*

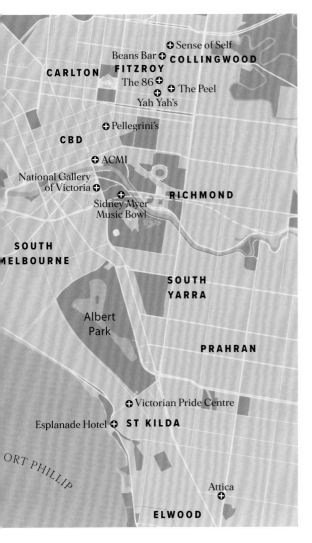

Sense of Self
Beans Bar
COLLINGWOOD
CARLTON
FITZROY
The 86
The Peel
Yah Yah's
Pellegrini's
CBD
ACMI
National Gallery
of Victoria
RICHMOND
Sidney Myer
Music Bowl
SOUTH
MELBOURNE
SOUTH
YARRA
Albert
Park
PRAHRAN
Victorian Pride Centre
Esplanade Hotel
ST KILDA
PORT PHILLIP
Attica
ELWOOD

WINING & DINING

"**Attica** is just outside of the city, and their wait-list can be anywhere from a few weeks to several months out. They have a set menu featuring this experimental Australian cuisine, using some out-there ingredients like emu or kangaroo.

"Other than that, I like to recommend **Pellegrini's**, an old Italian restaurant with a really homey feel.

"Also worth noting: it's a non-tipping culture, and the price you see is the price you pay—there are no additional taxes added afterward or anything."

FIRST-TIMER TIPS

"There are a lot of ticket inspectors on public transport and the fines are crazy. You would maybe pay $8 a day on a day-pass for public transport, but if you forget to buy one, you could get fined like $300. The alternative would be to Uber everywhere, but public transport tends to be less expensive and quicker.

"It's a 'dress however you want' vibe here. People definitely express their style openly. I'd say folks wear more black in Melbourne than in any other Australian city, especially in the colder months. But even in the heat, people will wear head-to-toe black. So that's the easiest way to look like a local."

More Places to Visit

....

Hares & Hyenas

Laird Hotel

MABU MABU

Pink Ember Studio

Pony Club Gym

Prince Public Bar

Railway Hotel South Melbourne

South of Johnston

Above: *Flamboyant and fabulous, Carnival takes to the São Paulo streets in February and March.*

São Paulo,
BRAZIL

RECOMMENDATIONS BY
Clovis Casemiro

KNOW BEFORE YOU GO
....

LANGUAGE
Portuguese

CURRENCY
Brazilian
Real (R$)

PRIDE CELEBRATIONS
Annually
between May
and June

WHEN TO GO
For drier, cooler
weather, June–
September;
for warmer,
wetter weather,
December–
March

A born-and-raised Paulista, **Clovis Casemiro** (he/him) has spent decades spreading the word about Brazil as a welcoming destination for the queer community. He began his career in tourism in 1979 and brought the **International LGBTQ+ Travel Association (IGLTA)** to Brazil in 1998, confident that LGBTQ+ tourism would generate positive visibility for his country.

"I tried to live in Miami. I tried to live in New York. But I didn't like to live there," Clovis said. "The US I love as a travel destination, but as for a place to live, São Paulo will always be best for me."

Today Clovis is responsible for IGLTA members in not just Brazil but Portugal and all of Latin America, continuing his lifelong efforts to build out these regions' reputations as inclusive places for queer travelers to visit with enthusiasm, not trepidation. But beyond that, Clovis has more than 25 years in LGBTQ+ tourism, so knows how to make travelers in that sector feel welcome.

"I tell people, it's like if you want to work with tourists who fish or tourists who golf. For the fishers, you need to be able to tell them where the river is and the kinds of fish they could catch. Golf is the same: you need to know if it's sand or if it's grass, 18 holes or nine holes, which are

the best courses nearby," he explained. "I tell them, think of LGBTQ+ tourism as the same— it's a segment you need to understand. Where would they want to go? What is the best time to go? It's not so different. It's a niche you need to know how to cater to."

While that approach applies to destinations worldwide, Clovis still thinks his home city is one of the best places for LGBTQ+ travelers to visit.

"Come to join us here," he urged. "You feel like you know the world when you visit São Paulo. We love to receive people, and gay people are very welcome here. We love to show off our city, and we have so many beautiful places to see."

SAFETY FIRST

"We have a lot of laws in Brazil that protect us. The most important one is against LGBTQ+ phobia. If you harass someone in the LGBTQ+ community in the street, at a restaurant, out shopping, you go to jail now. It's a federal law. From a small town in the Amazon to São Paulo city, it doesn't matter where you are.

"If you're at a bar as a gay couple and someone comes up to you and says, 'Oh, you can't kiss here, get out of here,' we have the **Dial 100 Service**. You call the number 100—it's a 24-hour service—and report if you experience anything like this, and they will help you right away. The police will protect LGBTQ+ people here. We cannot be discriminated against."

AN IDEAL DAY

"I'd start with a bakery in São Paulo for breakfast, something simple. We have **Padaria Bella Paulista** close to **Paulista Ave**, just one block away.

"From the bakery, we can go to the museum of photography called the **Instituto Moreira Salles**, or **IMS Paulista**. It's seven stories, all glass, more than 1200 sq meters [12,917 sq ft] with exhibition spaces, a cinema, a library of photos, a bookshop, and a restaurant. Admission here is free, too.

"Another of the most important museums for us near here is the **Museum of Art São Paulo**, or we call it **MASP**. It's a big, modern building, totally different from the rest of Paulista Ave.

When you go inside, you see works from Picasso or Monet, these big-name artists from all over the world. And of course, the work by Brazilian artists, too. MASP also has a restaurant called **A Baianeira**, one of the best places to eat on Paulista Ave.

"You can also take the subway, about one block from there, to the **República** stop. That's where you'll find our **Museu da Diversidade Sexual**, or **Museum of Sexual Diversity**, which focuses on the LGBTQ+ community in Brazil and how it has changed since the 1980s when we lost so many to AIDS.

"After that, we walk about 10 to 15 minutes and pass the **Teatro Municipal de São Paulo**, one of our city's architectural landmarks, which is amazing. It looks like something from Paris. Nearby is also our city hall and its **Edifício Matarazzo**, also known as the **Palácio do Anhangabaú**. They offer guided tours there for free about the architecture and the history of the building, and there's a gorgeous rooftop garden.

"I always recommend visitors make time to see the **Farol Santander**, owned by Santander bank. Some people call this São Paulo's Empire State Building, but we call it **Banespa** or **Banco do Estado de São Paulo**. On the 26th floor there is an observation deck with a panoramic view of the city. On the 21st floor, there is a skate park, thanks to a Brazilian professional skater called Bob Burnquist. But what is so unique here, to me, is in the basement, the **Bar do Cofre** (the 'Vault Bar'). You know those big safes from banks in the 1950s, the big door with the big handle that you spin? You go through this big door, and inside there is an incredible bar, like a speakeasy! If you go there in the afternoons or evenings, you can order cocktails and food, and it's like you're traveling in time to Brazil in the past."

*Above: Looking up at the Farol Santander, São Paulo's 'Empire State Building'; **Below:** Street art on Beco do Batman (Batman's Alley) in the Vila Madalena district.*

WINING & DINING

"For lunch, there's one special restaurant I like to take everyone called **Consulado Mineiro**, from Minas Gerais, named after a state of Brazil. The food is amazing. Beef, a lot of pork—the pork is very important to us in Brazil—black beans, rice, bananas, fried potatoes. I love it here because it's food from home. It's food I remember that feels like your grandmother could have made. And this is the place to order your caipirinhas; usually it's made with cachaça, that's our local brand of alcohol here, made from sugarcane. Or you can have a type of drink we call a caipiroska, which uses vodka instead.

The More You Know

"The subways in São Paulo are very big and very clean. Some stations have five or six floors, and there's art inside the subways."

"For dinner, you must go to **O Gato que Ri**, a small-catch restaurant from 1958. It's Brazilian and Italian cuisine. That's the best restaurant we can choose in São Paulo, believe me."

GAYBORHOODS

"It depends on the time of day. At about 3pm or 4pm in the afternoon, **Feira da Praça Benedito Calixto** is the place a lot of LGBTQ+ people go because here they have the bars, the outdoor markets, the shops. We go after lunch to enjoy a beer on the street. Then maybe have a nap during the hottest part of the day.

"At night, we go to **Largo do Arouche**, which is like the gay village. Here, we have small places like the **Cabarét da Cecília**; it's a small house, and they have three floors. The first floor is a live band. On the second floor, sometimes they have shows of beautiful girls dressing up—and beautiful boys dressing up—and dancing cabaret. The third floor is a bar where everyone dances together. It's just wonderful.

*Below: Caipirinhas are top of the São Paulo cocktail menu; **Opposite:** Take in LGBTQ+-focused displays at the city's Museum of Sexual Diversity.*

"We can enjoy various gay bars in this neighborhood, including the oldest in the country, **Caneca de Prata**. And if you're willing, weekends promise lots of parties at bars like **Eagle**, or parties for bears in particular at bars like **Bigger** or **Ursound**.

"If you like drag shows, we have another place close by called the **Blue Space**. They have beautiful drag shows—some of the drag queens there, they even competed for *RuPaul's Drag Race*! It's so nice. They have two or three different bars in this big house, so if you don't like drag shows, you can stay at the disco area and dance, or you can go to the bar. Personally, I'll be at the drag show."

UNIQUELY PAULISTA

"From Paulista Ave, you can take an inexpensive Uber ride to get to **Beco do Batman** (Batman's Alley), an area with lots of street art in the **Vila Madalena** area. Here, between **Rua Medeiros de Albuquerque** and **Rua Harmonia**, there are all of these graffiti designs in so many different colors, it's amazing. You can usually see not just Batman but Batwoman, even a gay Batman sometimes, and other characters from those comic books and movies.

"They have local beers in different bars nearby, and you can ask for a cup of cold beer and walk around with it, taking pictures of the Batman art, almost like an open-air art exhibition.

Most of the bars in São Paulo have beer on the sidewalk in the region of **Vieira de Carvalho**, **Largo do Arouche**, and **Rua Bento Freitas**, with easy walking distance between all kinds of different bars.

"From this Batman area, it's a short walk up a small hill to an area I love to go to: the **Antiques Fair**, or **Feira de Antiguidades**, which takes place on Sundays at Museum of Art São Paulo (MASP). It's a big square with lots of shopping and small street fairs for authentically Brazilian things—leather, or bags, or things like that. The modern shopping around there is so very nice, too."

FIRST-TIMER TIPS

"Buy a ticket from São Paulo to get to **Rio de Janeiro** while you're here. It's easy to get to. It's a one-hour flight, or you can go by bus in five hours. Normally people will go around 11pm at night to Rio and arrive there very early the next morning to spend the whole day on the beach.

"And aside from our annual Pride Parade in June, don't forget about **Carnival** in Brazil every February and March! Our gay community looks forward to this just as much as Pride, I think. For LGBTQ+ visitors, just choose anywhere—the city doesn't matter. We'll be there ready for you."

Opposite: São Paulo's Pride
Parade on Paulista Ave.

THE ULTIMATE LGBTQ+ TRAVEL HIT LIST

Whether you're seeking rest and relaxation or adventure and adrenaline rushes, inviting destinations beckon from all corners of the world to welcome queer explorers. Find inclusive travel inspiration for your next family vacation, couples retreat, solo adventure, or group trip, whatever your party's ages and interests may be.

Adrenaline-Pumping Adventures

For thrill-seekers, exhilarating experiences abound in inclusive destinations worldwide, from scorching deserts in the American Southwest to glistening glaciers in Iceland and beyond.

Whether the idea of scaling rock walls, biking through challenging terrain, or floating high above the desert gets your heart pumping, these iconic destinations offer thrilling backdrops for an unforgettable adventure.

BANFF, ALBERTA, CANADA

Known for its majestic mountains and almost otherworldly blue waters, Banff has long attracted all manner of outdoor adventurers.

Here among some of the highest mountain peaks in the **Canadian Rockies** you'll find the **Kicking Horse River** system, designated as a Canadian Heritage River and fed by glacial meltwater streams like **Otterhead** and **Beaverfoot**. Aside from astounding waterfalls like the **Takakkaw Falls** and **Wapta Falls**, this river has whitewater rapids ranging from class II to VI that flow along some of the Banff area's most remarkable landscapes.

Just minutes away in **Banff National Park** is **Banff Sunshine Village**, one of the most scenic ski resorts in North America. Here along the Continental Divide, at an altitude of 2195m (7200ft), are three mountains offering more than 13 sq km (5 sq miles) of skiable terrain for skiers of all levels. The most extreme adventurers will want to make their way to the infamous **Delirium Dive**, a hair-raisingly steep free-ride zone named one of the most extreme ski runs in the world.

Those new to thrill-seeking can make their way to **Mt Norquay's via ferrata**—Italian for 'iron road'—for a hands-on climbing experience featuring steel cables and iron rungs embedded right into the mountain. This guided ascent is an ideal opportunity for those without prior climbing experience to safely scale the cliffs above

Above: *Aptly named Emerald Lake in Yoho National Park, Canadian Rockies.*

Mt Norquay and marvel at some of the best bird's-eye views of Banff National Park, with the option to choose from five different routes ranging from two to six hours.

Alternatively, consider descending with a caving tour of **Rat's Nest Cave**, one of Canada's longest caves, offering a maze of over 4km (2.5 miles) of chambers and passageways. Crawl through tight spaces and slide into caverns completely untouched by sunlight at this designated Provincial Historic Site, but know that there are no artificial lights, handrails, or boardwalks to guide you through your journey. You've been warned.

CAIRNS, QUEENSLAND, AUSTRALIA

Whether underwater, in the air, or on the ground, the laid-back city of Cairns in **Tropical North Queensland** is the setting for unforgettable adventures to some of Australia's most stunning natural attractions.

The area is lauded as a gateway to a once-in-a-lifetime excursion for the bulk of travelers living outside of Oceania: scuba diving the **Great Barrier Reef**, the world's largest coral-reef complex and one of the Seven Wonders of the Natural World, where vibrant coral cays and more than 3000 individual reef systems offer an unparalleled underwater experience.

Venturing from the sea to the sky, leap into the lush rainforests of **Smithfield** at one of the most epic bungy jumps in Australia, the **AJ Hackett Bungy Jump**, a spine-tingling 50m (164ft) drop above a deep natural lagoon with phenomenal views of the world heritage rainforest at **Barron Gorge National Park**. Or fly through the treetops of the **Daintree Forest** with a **Jungle Surfing Canopy Tour**, zipping above branches with the birds through what's thought to be the oldest living rainforest on Earth.

Right: Skiing Coronet Peak in Queenstown, New Zealand/Aotearoa; Opposite: Fiordland National Park in New Zealand's Southern Alps.

For more hands-on thrills, explore the muddy trails of North Queensland on a quad bike at **Blazing Saddles**, navigating through the smattering of creeks and winding rainforest paths at **Yorkeys Knob**. Or take to the **Coral Sea** at Yorkeys Knob's beaches, where the perfect conditions for kitesurfing offer ample opportunities for high-speed excitement on the water.

MOAB, UTAH, USA

A playground for adrenaline seekers, Moab is home to some of the United States' most scenic vistas, from the red-rock formations of **Arches National Park** to the mesas and buttes of **Canyonlands National Park** and the powerful white-water rapids of the **Colorado River**, ranging from class I to class IV.

Moab is also world-famous for its mountain biking, and the **Slickrock Trail** is one of its most popular rides. Don't let the trail's 16km (10-mile) length fool you; with challenging terrains and steep inclines, this highly technical ride is equal parts exasperating and exhilarating. Those brave enough to attempt it can expect something of a self-guided roller-coaster ride, crossing the rugged expanse of the **Navajo Sandstone** desert's petrified sand dunes before turning parallel to the **Colorado River** and descending toward an expanse of—you guessed it—slickrock.

The sandstone formations in and around Moab lend themselves nicely to both rock climbing and bouldering. Particularly in areas like **Wall Street**—a roadside crag and towering 150m-high (500ft) cliff looming above **Potash Rd** and running along the Colorado River—climbers can find routes for all skill levels, with gorgeous views of the expansive desert and the river's rapids below.

If that's not exciting enough, consider canyoneering: an adventure offered by local tour companies combining hiking, rappelling, and sometimes swimming to allow visitors to explore staggering slot canyons that are otherwise inaccessible, like **Bow and Arrow Canyon** or **Elephant Butte Canyon**.

The truly fearless might even consider joining the throngs of dedicated highliners crossing Moab's canyons—like its infamous **Fruit Bowl** near **Mineral Bottom Rd**—on slacklines rigged up

Left: *Bungy-jumping from New Zealand/Aotearoa's Kawarau Bridge, an iconic Queenstown site.*

to 90m (300ft) above the ground: it's a thrilling balancing act that's not for the faint of heart.

QUEENSTOWN, NEW ZEALAND/AOTEAROA

Often dubbed the 'Adventure Capital of the World,' Queenstown is home to all manner of action-movie-worthy activities, but it all started with bungy jumping.

The heart-stopping leap over the **Kawarau River** has been drawing visitors from around the world in droves for decades. So many, in fact, that they've expanded the operation to include other scream-inducing options, like arcing a whopping 300m (984ft) and back on the **Nevis Swing**, propelling 150m (492ft) across the **Nevis Valley** at 100km/h (62mph) in 1.5 seconds with the **Nevis Catapult**, or speeding down the 130m (427ft) **Kawarau Zipride** at 60km/h (37mph).

Adventurers can also go jet-boating on the **Shotover River**, twisting and turning with high-speed maneuvers through the narrow **Shotover Canyons**, combining speed and spins with breathtaking scenery for a unique water-based thrill.

Those who prefer cold-weather excursions can try their hand at heli-skiing, for unique access to untouched snow in remote mountain locations in the heart of the **Southern Alps**—ideal for skiers and snowboarders looking to push their limits and experience the best powder away from crowded slopes.

REYKJAVÍK, ICELAND

Isolated Iceland is at the top of many an adventurer's to-do list, and for good reason. The raw beauty of the island's unique and distinctly varied biomes offers awe-inspiring—and often perilous—panoramic views at every turn, from volcanic black-sand beaches to thundering waterfalls and beyond.

Head southeast from the capital, Rekjavík, along the southern region of Iceland's famous **Ring Road** is the **Sólheimajökull Glacier**, an outlet glacier where intrepid travelers can hike across the icy landscapes that make up part of the larger **Mýrdalsjökull Glacier**. But don't let the serene, hypnotically blue ice formations lull you into a false sense of security as you explore this frozen feature—deadly glacial crevasses and black holes can sneak up on inexperienced hikers at any moment. So, this thrill is best enjoyed with an ice axe and set of crampons for safe glacier walking, *and* an experienced glacier guide leading the way.

For an even more thrilling glacial exploration, sign up for a snowmobiling tour of **Langjökull Glacier**, where a guide will take you speeding across the white expanse of Iceland's second-largest glacier. Or experience Iceland's volcanic landscape from the inside by caving in one of its many lava tubes, like the magnificent lava tunnel **Raufarhólshellir**, formed by flowing lava and offering a look into the geological forces that shaped this island nation.

If you're keen to explore the waters surrounding the island, hop onto a fast-paced rigid inflatable boat (RIB) and speed out into the Atlantic Ocean to see Iceland's marine wildlife, such as whales and dolphins,) in their natural habitat. Or dive into the crystal-clear waters of the **Silfra Fissure**, located in the **Þingvellir National Park**, a rift formed between the North American and Eurasian tectonic plates, where you can swim between continents, snorkeling in some of the clearest water anywhere in the world.

Right: The view to Aoraki/Mt Cook from Hooker Lake in New Zealand's Southern Alps; *Opposite:* Lakagígar volcanic fissure in Vatnajökull National Park, Iceland.

Awe-Inspiring Art

For centuries, art has been a powerful tool for social change and activism, offering marginalized communities a unique opportunity to raise awareness, challenge stereotypes, and advocate for their rights. For queer art aficionados seeking inspiration and immersion in diverse artistic landscapes, consider these captivating destinations where LGBTQ+ art flourishes.

BARCELONA, SPAIN

You can hardly bring up Barcelona without someone mentioning the architectural wonders of Antoni Gaudí, from the **Sagrada Família** to the **Casa Batlló** to **Park Güell**. In fairness, the Catalan Modernista blended Art Nouveau, Gothic, and organic forms to create surreal and fantastical works that truly must be seen to be believed.

But Gaudí was far from the only artist in **Catalonia** with a unique approach to his work. Pablo Picasso also called Barcelona home for nine formative years of his adolescence and academic training, and developed a strong emotional bond with the city. That is why you can find his earliest works from these years in Barcelona at the **Picasso Museum**. Paintings like the *Roof of Barcelona* and the *Portrait of Aunt Pepa*, some of the 20th century's most influential and unique works of art, are now housed in a series of medieval palaces in the city's **Barri Gòtic** (Gothic Quarter).

Barcelona was also the birthplace of Catalan painter, sculptor, and ceramist Joan Miró. At the **Fundació Joan Miró**, you can immerse yourself in the surreal world of Miró's work: 217 paintings, 178 sculptures, nine textiles, four ceramics, an estimated 8000 drawings, and nearly all of his prints.

There are also other stunning cultural hot spots like the **Museu d'Art Contemporani de Barcelona** (MACBA), the **Centre de Cultura Contemporània de Barcelona**, and the **CaixaForum**, not to mention the colorful murals and urban art installations in vibrant neighborhoods like **Raval** and **Poblenou**.

But there's more to take in throughout Barcelona than just the visual arts—like world-class operas and ballets at the esteemed **Liceu Theater** and live musical performances at the **Palau de la Música Catalana**, a UNESCO World Heritage Site and one of Barcelona's most stylish concert halls. The Palau was designed by Lluís Domènech i Montaner, with intricate stained-glass windows and breathtaking mosaics.

BUENOS AIRES, ARGENTINA

A cosmopolitan South American city known for its rich cultural diversity and vibrant arts scene, Buenos Aires has a long-standing tradition of nurturing artistic talent and

Above: *Barcelona, framed by a curving, mosaic-covered balcony at Antoni Gaudí's Park Güell.*

community—and LGBTQ+ artists in particular have played a significant role in shaping the city's artistic landscape.

Take the **Museo de Arte Latinoamericano de Buenos Aires (Malba)**, home to an extensive collection of modern and contemporary Latin American art, including works by LGBTQ+ artists such as Frida Kahlo, Xul Solar, and David LaChapelle. Or the **Museo Nacional de Bellas Artes**, nearly bursting with European and Argentine art created by renowned artists such as Goya, Rembrandt, and Van Gogh, as well as Argentine masters like Xul Solar and Benito Quinquela Martín.

Both of these institutions have contributed to the reputation Buenos Aires has earned as a hub of creativity and expression among queer art aficionados, as have the city's LGBTQ+ art galleries. The **Espacio G**, **Hormigas Negras**, and **Galería Mar Dulce** feature diverse artworks ranging in media—from painting and sculpture to photography and more—in celebration of queer identity and expression.

But in Buenos Aires, art goes beyond that which can be seen—or even that which can be heard, like performances at the grand opera house **Teatro Colón**, an architectural masterpiece with world-class acoustics.

At **Tango Queer Milonga**—dance events hosted by LGBTQ+ tango communities in Buenos Aires—art demands to be physically felt. Experience the passion and sensuality of Argentine tango, embracing the inclusive and nonbinary ethos of the queer tango movement, which invites dancers of all genders and orientations to dance the night away to traditional tango music.

For those not ready to hit the dance floor, Buenos Aires regularly plays host to book readings, author talks, poetry slams, and more at LGBTQ+-friendly bookstores and cultural spaces like **Librería de Ávila** and **Casa Rainbow**, where works by LGBTQ+ writers and poets challenge stereotypes and amplify queer voices. Or you can time your travels to coincide with the **Buenos Aires International Festival of Independent Cinema**, where groundbreaking films, documentaries, and shorts explore LGBTQ+ themes and narratives.

Whatever you do, don't miss your chance to see the historic **Casa Rosada** and **Plaza de Mayo**, where queer Argentine activists have gathered for decades to protest for equality and human rights.

Opposite: *Argentina's Museo de Arte Latinoamericano de Buenos Aires (Malba), a light-filled showcase for modern art.*

MONTRÉAL, QUÉBEC, CANADA

Home to some of Canada's premier art institutions, such as the **Montréal Museum of Fine Arts** and the **Montréal Museum of Contemporary Art**, this Quebecois metropolis is a haven for art lovers of any orientation—but especially for LGBTQ+ travelers looking to immerse themselves in a world of creative wonder.

Queer art exhibitions beckon at welcoming venues like **Galerie Artefact**, **Arsenal Contemporary Art**, and **Never Apart**, while urban art installations celebrating queer culture and history pop up all over public spaces in inclusive neighborhoods like the **Gay Village**, **Plateau-Mont-Royal**, and **Mile End**.

To say Montréal was built upon a foundation of artistic expression wouldn't be an exaggeration—its **Underground City** is certainly proof of that. This vast network of pedestrian tunnels, shops, and metro stations is adorned with murals and sculptures. Sign up for a guided tour to learn the history and culture of this unique city-beneath-a-city and to discover hidden artworks throughout the subterranean maze.

Back above ground, browse LGBTQ+-inspired books and magazines at queer-friendly Montréal bookstores and cafes like **Librairie Drawn & Quarterly** and **Café Rendezvous**; or explore the stalls at the historic **Atwater Market** and peruse locally crafted jewelry, ceramics, textiles, and other artisanal goods created by Montréal-based artists.

If you'd rather try your hand at crafting art of your own, consider a visit to **Atelier Circulaire**, a renowned printmaking studio where you can learn traditional techniques and create your own unique prints under the guidance of experienced printmakers.

For an unforgettable evening, enjoy some classical music at the **Maison Symphonique** concert hall, where the talented musicians of the **Montréal Symphony Orchestra** are led by renowned conductor Kent Nagano in performances of symphonies, operas, and chamber music. Or catch a play or musical at LGBTQ+ theaters like **La Chapelle Scènes Contemporaines** or **Théâtre Sainte-Catherine**, both dedicated to promoting LGBTQ+ visibility and representation in the arts.

Left: *Colorful Plateau-Mont-Royal is just one of the inclusive neighborhoods in marvelous Montréal, Canada.*

SEOUL, SOUTH KOREA

From ancient architectural relics steeped in tradition to neoteric renderings of a Seoulite future, the artistic endeavors in the South Korean capital city manage to transcend both space and time while holding viewers and visitors firmly in the present.

At the **Dongdaemun Design Plaza** sits the world's largest three-dimensional atypical building: a futuristic four-story spaceship made with more than 45,000 aluminum panels and amorphous concrete and designed by the late Zaha Hadid, the first female architect to win the Pritzker Prize. This multicultural complex plays host to more than 100 cultural events each year, ranging from fashion shows to art exhibitions and beyond, in addition to welcoming visitors to its own **DDP Museum**, **Design Showroom**, and **Design Store**.

On the other end of Seoul's space-time continuum is the **Bukchon Hanok Village**, a historic neighborhood known for its *hanok (*well-preserved traditional Korean houses). Many of these *hanok* have been converted into art galleries, studios, and cultural spaces—like the **Bukchon Art Museum**, **the Han Sangsu Embroidery Museum**, **the Bukchon Photo Museum**, and the **Bukchon Cultural Center**—where visitors can admire traditional Korean art, crafts, and performances while experiencing the charm of old Seoul.

More contemporary works from queer Korean artists await at the **Seoul Museum of Art** and in LGBTQ+-friendly galleries and event spaces like **Gallery Mspace** or **Artspace Hue**. In **Hongdae**, Seoul's hip and artsy neighborhood, an indie art scene continues to blossom, with street art and performance spaces showcasing the work of emerging artists, including LGBTQ+ creators pushing the boundaries of expression and identity. Queer-friendly cafes like **PRISM** and **Cafe Unicorn** feature LGBTQ+

artwork in addition to hosting events and performances by queer artists, providing a safe and inclusive environment for artistic expression and community building.

Each year, the **Seoul Queer Culture Festival** celebrates the LGBTQ+ community and its contributions to Korean culture through art, music, films, and performances, offering a platform for queer artists to showcase their talents and advocate for equality and acceptance. Consider planning a visit during this annual summer celebration—or during the **Seoul International Queer Film Festival**, which takes place each year in July or August.

SYDNEY, NEW SOUTH WALES, AUSTRALIA

A visit to Sydney is a no-brainer for artistic travelers—if nothing else, for a trip to the architectural marvel that is the **Sydney Opera House**. For exclusive access to behind-the-scenes areas of this iconic landmark, consider booking a backstage tour before you attend a performance there, to learn about its history, architecture, and inner workings while exploring rehearsal rooms, dressing rooms, and backstage areas.

Architecture buffs will also be delighted to discover Sydney's rich Art Deco heritage with a guided walking tour of the city's architectural gems from the 1920s and 1930s. Learn about the design principles and cultural influences that shaped the Art Deco movement in Sydney with visits to historic buildings like the **QVB**, **State Theatre**, and the former **Daily Telegraph** building.

Right: Fantastical Gyeongui Line Book Street in Seoul, South Korea; *Opposite:* The traditional Bukchon Hanok Village and Seoul city skyline.

Explore art exhibitions and gallery shows at inclusive venues like the **National Art School Gallery**, **Museum of Contemporary Art Australia**, and the **Australian Centre for Photography**—not to mention one of Australia's top art institutions, the **Art Gallery of New South Wales**, which houses an extensive collection of works from Australian artists and more.

See boundary-pushing performances by gender-bending artists and drag performers at venues like the **Red Rattler Theatre** and the **Imperial Hotel**, where shows challenge gender roles and the notion of identity, celebrating the beauty and diversity of queer expression.

Make your way to **Cockatoo Island**, a UNESCO World Heritage Site in **Sydney Harbour**, which hosts several contemporary art exhibitions throughout the year. The island's industrial history provides a striking backdrop for large-scale artworks and immersive installations alike.

If you're lucky enough to visit Sydney in the late springtime—October through November, in the southern hemisphere—you can also check out **Sculpture by the Sea**, one of the world's largest outdoor sculpture exhibitions. Hosted along the coastline between **Bondi Beach** and **Tamarama Beach**, this annual open-air gallery features more than 100 sculptures crafted by artists from around the world, standing against the backdrop of the Pacific Ocean.

Any time of year, you can participate in hands-on artisan workshops at **Carriageworks**, a contemporary multi-arts precinct based in a historic railway-carriage workshop. Skilled local craftspeople teach traditional skills like pottery, weaving, and printmaking, so you can create your own unique artwork to bring home as a souvenir.

Opposite: Australia's landmark
Sydney Opera House, designed by
Danish architect Jørn Utzon.

Family-Friendly Festivities

For LGBTQ+ families, choosing the ideal vacation destination goes beyond just beautiful scenery and fun activities for all ages. It's about finding a place where everyone in the family feels welcome and able to truly be themselves.

These unforgettable experiences offer a safe, inclusive environment where LGBTQ+ families can create cherished memories together.

CHICAGO, ILLINOIS, USA

The US state of Illinois has strong legal protections for the queer community, including laws that safeguard residents and travelers alike from discrimination. Chicago, in particular, is home to a thriving queer community, including one of America's best-known LGBTQ+ enclaves, the **Boystown** neighborhood, a Lakeview area that's home to a plethora of queer-owned businesses and cultural institutions aimed at kids and adults alike.

Located on the shore of Lake Michigan, Chicago's **Museum Campus** is home to several world-class museums that cater to families. At the **Field Museum**, discover ancient artifacts, dinosaur skeletons, and interactive exhibits. Visit the **Adler Planetarium** to journey through space and explore the wonders of the universe through immersive astronomical exhibits. Explore aquatic life from around the globe at the **Shedd Aquarium**.

To see the city from a different perspective, make your way to **Navy Pier** and climb aboard the impressive **Centennial Wheel**, where you can enjoy breathtaking views of the Chicago skyline from your seat on the 60m-high (196ft) Ferris wheel. Throughout the rest of **Pier Park**, keep the thrills coming with rides on the spinning teacups, high-flying wave swinger, historic musical carousel, and more.

Then make your way to **Portillo's**, the go-to place for a traditional Chicago-style hot dog with all the fixings; or to **Giordano's**, a family-friendly restaurant (with locations throughout the city) where you can try their famous stuffed deep-dish pizza. For dessert, head to **Margie's Candies** in **Logan Square** for a hot-fudge sundae in a nostalgic setting.

No visit to Chicago would be complete without a trip to **Millennium Park** to get a family selfie in the famous **Cloud Gate** sculpture, better known as the 'Bean.' Wander through the beautiful **Lurie Garden** for a brief, peaceful escape from the city's hustle and bustle. In the warmer months, cool off in the interactive **Crown Fountain**, featuring digital projections of resident Chicagoans' faces.

COPENHAGEN, DENMARK

As the first country in the world to legally recognize same-sex partnerships, Denmark has been treating LGBTQ+ families equally under the law since 1989. It's consistently ranked one of the safest countries in the world, making its vibrant capital city of Copenhagen an excellent choice for LGBTQ+ families.

There are so many family-friendly attractions in Copenhagen that it might be hard to choose one, but **Tivoli Gardens** is a must-visit. Located right in the heart of the city, it's the world's second-oldest amusement park, with manicured gardens, dozens of rides and roller-coasters, open-air theaters featuring ballet and theater performances, and so many restaurant options that even the pickiest of eaters are guaranteed to be pleased.

Families visiting during the summer months can relax and unwind at **Amager Beach Park**, Copenhagen's urban beach, where you can swim in the clean, cool waters and soak up some sunshine in a safe, welcoming environment. Along the way, don't miss the photo op with the iconic **Little Mermaid Statue** along the waterfront,

Above: Close encounters with stingrays at Copenhagen's Den Blå Planet aquarium, Denmark.

a beloved symbol of the city's culture inspired by the classic Hans Christian Andersen fairy tale.

Adventurers of all ages can still marvel at colorful marine life at **Den Blå Planet**, Denmark's national aquarium and the largest aquarium in Northern Europe. Aside from oohing and ahhing over the thousands of creatures from an underwater tunnel, kiddos can learn while they play at the **Water Playground**, where pumps and drains demonstrate the various ways that water can be used.

Leave time for a visit to the **Copenhagen Zoo** to see not just lions but over 4000 other animals, representing more than 250 different species.

PALM SPRINGS, CALIFORNIA, USA

Active families will relish the opportunity to explore the stunning desert landscapes, sunny weather, and vibrant LGBTQ+ community in this inclusive destination in Southern California.

Outdoor adventures abound at **Joshua Tree National Park**, from nature walks and easy hikes to rock climbing and stargazing. Trails like the **Hidden Valley Nature Trail**, **Barker Dam Trail**, and **Cholla Cactus Garden Trail** offer relatively flat terrain and the chance to see desert flora and fauna up close, from bighorn sheep to desert tortoises and more. Older kids and grown-ups can try rock climbing on the park's renowned rock formations, experiencing Joshua Tree's unique geology firsthand. Or visit the park after dark, when its remote location and minimal light pollution make it an excellent spot for observing the night sky.

For a more leisurely climb, families can take a ride on the world's largest rotating tramcar, the **Palm Springs Aerial Tramway**, and ascend to the top of **Mt San Jacinto** for panoramic views of the desert below. Alternatively, opt to descend rather than ascend and explore the stunning natural beauty of the **Indian Canyons**.

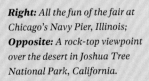

Right: All the fun of the fair at Chicago's Navy Pier, Illinois;
Opposite: *A rock-top viewpoint over the desert in Joshua Tree National Park, California.*

Discover ancient rock formations, hike scenic trails, and cool off in the refreshing streams and waterfalls at **Palm Canyon**, **Andreas Canyon**, and **Murray Canyon**.

Marvel at cacti, succulents, and other desert plants from around the world at the enchanting **Moorten Botanical Garden**, or dive into aviation history at the **Palm Springs Air Museum**, home to a vast collection of vintage aircraft, exhibits about restored planes and aviation technology, and inspiring stories of pilots' courage and heroism.

If you have the chance to visit Palm Springs on a Thursday evening, don't miss out on the vibrant energy at **VillageFest**, a weekly street fair along **Palm Canyon Dr** featuring live entertainment, local vendors galore, and delicious samples of local Southern California cuisine.

TORONTO, ONTARIO, CANADA

Consistently ranked one of the world's safest and most LGBTQ+-friendly travel destinations, Toronto is an excellent place to plan a vacation packed full of fun for the whole family.

Kick off your trip with a **Toronto Islands Ferry Cruise** to get the lay of the land (and the water), enjoying panoramic views of the city's skyline and waterfront, snapping photos of famous landmarks, and learning about Toronto's rich history and architecture from knowledgeable local guides.

Within those Toronto Islands, make your way to **Centre Island** and you'll find the **Centreville Amusement Park**. Glide through the clouds on the Sky Ride chairlift, bounce into each other in Bumper Boats, or take a spin on the antique carousel, the only Dentzel Menagerie Carousel left in Canada and one of only a handful left in the world. End your adventure with a sweet treat from **O'Bumbles Ice Cream Parlour** or **Mr Flipp's Popcorn Wagon**.

Back on the mainland, if weather allows, go for a family paddleboat ride across **Zoo and Grenadier Pond** at **High Park**, Toronto's largest public park. Kids can climb, slide, and engage

Left: Toronto's Royal Ontario Museum, home to a wealth of kid-friendly interactive exhibits.

their imaginations at **Jamie Bell Adventure Playground**, featuring castle structures, suspension bridges, and sandy play areas to inspire their adventures.

For indoor entertainment and education, visit the world-renowned **Royal Ontario Museum** to enjoy hands-on galleries where kids can touch real artifacts, try on period costumes, and take part in interactive experiences that bring the region's culture and history to life.

Art aficionados can admire masterpieces at the **Art Gallery of Ontario**, one of the largest art museums in North America, where visitors of all ages can participate in family-friendly art-making activities and explore interactive exhibits at the AGO Kids Gallery. Or visit the Dinosaur Gallery to learn about prehistoric life on Earth and see the skeletons of ancient dinosaurs.

Animal lovers can explore underwater habitats of more than 20,000 different creatures, from jellyfish to stingrays and more, at **Ripley's Aquarium of Canada**, and walk through glass tunnels surrounded by marine life.

Those who prefer land-based animal experiences won't want to miss the **Toronto Zoo**, where kids can embark on wildlife adventures and explore immersive exhibits like the Gorilla Rainforest, the Tundra Trek, and the Discovery Zone, participating in animal encounters and education programs promoting conservation and biodiversity.

WELLINGTON, NEW ZEALAND/AOTEAROA

New Zealand has long been a pioneer of LGBTQ+ rights, and Wellington in particular is known for its progressive and inclusive culture where diversity is celebrated and embraced year-round. The city is home to ample queer-friendly experiences that are not just welcoming but fun for the whole family.

Start with a family day at one of the many beaches around Wellington. If you're traveling with younger children, head to **Oriental Bay**, an urban beach on the inner harbor with golden sands shipped in from Golden Bay on the South Island and calm waters that are ideal for younger swimmers. For those who enjoy water sports, **Paraparaumu** on the **Kapiti Coast** is the ideal starting point for kayaking, paddleboarding, or chartering a cruise. Surfers can head to **Lyall Bay** for ideal wind and wave conditions. For year-round swimming and sunbathing, look no further than **Scorching Bay**, just a short way from Wellington's city center on the **Miramar Peninsula**.

Movie buffs can't miss the chance to take a guided tour at the Academy Award–winning **Wētā Workshop**, where you can learn about the making of movie effects for *The Lord of the Rings*, *Avatar*, *The Chronicles of Narnia*, *King Kong*, and more.

Have your own *Willy Wonka and the Chocolate Factory* sort of experience at the **Wellington Chocolate Factory**, where kids do not just learn about the chocolate-making process; they also get to decorate their own milk-chocolate bar and create their own custom wrapper. In addition, kids can enjoy a Wellington Chocolate Factory hot chocolate and plenty of free chocolate samples along the way.

Ride the **Wellington Cable Car** up to the **Wellington Botanic Garden** as the sun sets, then make your way to the Main Garden after dark for the chance to see the rare New Zealand glowworms shining in the night. From there, you can walk over to **Space Place** to be mesmerized by its full-dome planetarium.

Right: Ride the cable car to the Botanic Garden and planetarium in Wellington, New Zealand/Aotearoa; *Opposite:* Living the best (van)life in Joshua Tree National Park, USA.

Inclusive Island Escapes

From the pulsating beats of Ibiza's nightlife to the tranquil shores of Mykonos, these enchanting destinations have plenty more to offer than just sun-kissed beaches and azure seas.

CANARY ISLANDS, SPAIN

Southwest of the Iberian Peninsula you'll find the Canary Islands, an autonomous community of Spain spread across seven main islands and a smattering of smaller islands and islets. Though just 100km (62 miles) west of the African mainland, the Canary Islands are an integral part of Spain, recognizing Spanish as their official language and adopting predominantly Spanish cultures and customs.

With year-round warm weather, the Canary Islands are a paradise for beach lovers of all persuasions. **Gran Canaria** is often regarded as the most LGBTQ+-friendly island in the Canaries—particularly the capital city of **Las Palmas** and beloved beach **Playa de las Canteras**. While you've probably already heard of this island's famous **Maspalomas Pride** celebration, Gran Canaria also plays host to LGBTQ+ events throughout the year and has a vibrant nightlife scene at **Yumbo Centrum**, an LGBTQ+ shopping center in resort town **Playa del Inglés**.

On **Tenerife**, you'll find a particularly queer-friendly atmosphere in the areas around **Playa de las Américas** and **Puerto de la Cruz**, where resorts and beaches are considered inclusive by default. Drag shows at the **Babylon Disco Gay Pub** are always entertaining. Tenerife is also home to **Mt Teide**, Spain's highest peak, and surrounding **Teide National Park**. Take a cable car up the mountain for breathtaking panoramic vistas.

Though the LGBTQ+ scene on **Lanzarote** isn't quite as extensive as those on Gran Canaria or Tenerife, this island still offers a welcoming environment and queer-friendly accommodations, especially in the resort areas of **Puerto del Carmen** and **Playa Blanca**. Outdoorsy travelers shouldn't miss the otherworldly landscape of volcanic craters, lava fields, and geothermal geysers at **Timanfaya National Park**.

GREEK ISLANDS

Though there are around 6000 Greek islands in total, only about 200 of them have a resident population.

Of the inhabited islands, the Greek getaway best known for LGBTQ+ friendliness is **Mykonos**; its vibrant queer scene has a long history of catering specifically to LGBTQ+ travelers. For crystal-clear waters, sand, and sunshine, you can't beat gay beaches **Elia Beach** and **Paraga Beach**. If you're seeking laid-back food and drink spots, look no further than **Kastro's Bar**. **Elysium Bar** is the best spot for craft cocktails and stunning sunsets. For partying until sunrise, hot spots

Babylon and **JackieO' Beach Club** are right next door to one another at **Super Paradise Beach**, and are two of the most popular gay clubs on the island.

In **Crete**, the cities of **Iraklio (Heraklion)**, **Rethymno**, and **Hania (Chania)** are known for welcoming queer travelers. But the heart of the LGBTQ+ scene in Crete is **Hersonissos**, where you can find Crete's only exclusive gay bar, **YOLO Pub**, in addition to plenty of queer-friendly entertainment at venues like **Cameo Club**, **New York Beach Club**, and **Club Sensation**. Soak up the sun at **Sarandaris Beach** or **Kommos Beach**, both nudist beaches frequented by gay travelers. Lace up your hiking books and explore the rugged landscapes of the **Lefka Ori** (White Mountains), with trails and routes for hikers of all levels. Or discover the ancient Minoan ruins of **Knossos Palace** near Iraklio, one of the most important archaeological sites in Greece and the center of Minoan civilization.

Last but not least, there's **Lesbos**, home of the ancient Greek poet Sappho and to a population of around 85,000 residents known as Lesbians—unaffiliated with the LGBTQ+ identity by the same name, though the island is home to one of the world's

Above: Mt Teide, towering over the surrounding *Teide National Park in Tenerife, Canary Islands.*

only lesbian villages (and yes, we're talking about gay women this time), **Skala Eressos**. This under-the-radar destination is home to a slew of women-only hotels and a sense of restful acceptance that can be hard to find as a female traveler at any age. Skala Eressos, like the rest of Lesbos, is a paradise for birdwatchers. With more than 300 bird species recorded on the island, Lesbos is actually one of the best bird-watching destinations in all of Europe. The island is also home to a UNESCO World Heritage Site and one of the largest and best-preserved petrified forests in the world: the **Petrified Forest of Lesbos**, with fossilized trees dating back millions of years.

JAPANESE ISLANDS

While LGBTQ+-friendly spaces aren't necessarily as prevalent in Japan as they are in some other countries, it's not hard to find welcoming environments as a queer traveler in this beautiful country if you know where to look.

Located on the island of **Honshū**, the country's capital city of **Tokyo** is typically considered the most queer-friendly city in Japan, particularly in **Shinjuku Ni-chome**—or 'Nicho' for short—which is known as the gay district. Gay men can grab a drink at **Aiiro Cafe** or **Dragon Men**, while lesbians flock to **Dorobune**. Queer visitors of all identities can enjoy laid-back vibes at **Cafe & Bar Donyoku** or **Shinjuku Building**, or see comedy and drag shows at **Tokyo Closet Ball** or **Campy**. Order fresh sushi and sashimi from local vendors at **Tsukiji Outer Market**, or visit neighborhoods **Ebisu** or **Kanda** to check out the city's local breweries and craft beer bars. Make your way to Tokyo's oldest temple, **Sensō-ji**, and explore its vibrant **Nakamise Shopping Street** and historic main mall.

Also located on Honshū, the city of **Osaka** is known for its own gay district, the **Doyama-cho** area in **Umeda**. Lauded as Osaka's 'gayest' bar, tiny and perpetually packed venue **Frenz Frenzy** takes tremendous pride in having been a stop on

*Right: Looking down onto the lesbian village of Skala Eressos on Lesbos, in the Greek islands; **Opposite:** Boating the moat around the Osaka-jō castle on Honshū island, Japan.*

Lady Gaga's Monster Ball tour in 2009. Visitors can expect strong drinks, psychedelic disco decor, and always-available free karaoke. **G Physique** and **Explosion** are two more of Osaka's friendliest gay bars, if you're looking to make it a bar crawl. Explore the street-food stalls in **Dōtombori**, Osaka's buzzing entertainment district. Or take a scenic cruise along **Osaka Bay** for dramatic views of the city's skyline, historic landmarks, and waterfront.

MEDITERRANEAN ISLANDS

Bordered by Europe to the north, Africa to the south, and Asia to the east, the Mediterranean Sea is home to islands spread across a variety of regions and cultures, each with its own unique atmosphere and charm.

Perhaps the queer-friendliest among them is **Ibiza**, one of the **Balearic Islands** situated off the eastern coast of Spain. Pronounced with the signature Spanish lisp, Ibi*th*a is known for its plethora of gay beaches, including the popular **Playa Es Cavallet**, with its clothing-optional areas, as well as **Cala Comte** and **Cala Salada**. Neighborhoods **Dalt Vila** (also known as Ibiza Old Town) and **Sant Antoni de Portmany** are known for LGBTQ+-friendly venues like legendary nightclub **Pacha**, which hosts queer parties and events year-round. For astonishing sunsets, the legendary **Café del Mar** in Sant Antoni is a must. For those seeking something a little steamier, **Sauna Bruc** is a welcoming option for queer travelers in need of a spa day.

Left: Pink-sand perfection on Ibiza's Cala Comte, one of the island's many gay beaches.

Leisurely Locales

Indulge in the lap of leisure and luxury in these restful and relaxing vacation destinations: hot springs in Japan, a beachfront massage in Thailand, and wine tasting in the picturesque Italian countryside.

HAKONE, JAPAN

Begin your journey in Japan communing with nature. Join a *shinrin-yoku*—a forest bathing session—led by certified instructors, and where you'll unwind to connect with the natural world through mindfulness practices and sensory exploration on a guided nature walk along the trails of the **Hakone-Yumoto**.

Climb aboard a cruise on nearby **Lake Ashi**, a crater lake surrounded by forested hills and volcanic peaks, with breathtaking views of **Mt Fuji** as well as the **Hakone** city skyline. End your tour with a visit to the **Hakone Shrine**, where you can pay your respects at sacred sites, admire Shinto art and architecture, and participate in rituals and ceremonies if time allows.

Take to the skies above the city on the **Hakone Ropeway**, a scenic cable car that offers breathtaking vistas of Hakone's volcanic landscape. Traveling from **Sounzan** to **Ōwakudani**, you can see all the way down to the bottom of the valley below you. On the way to **Tōgendai** you get gorgeous views of Lake Ashi and, on a clear day, you can even catch a glimpse of Mt Fuji.

Hakone is famously a haven for *onsen* (hot springs), with hundreds of baths to choose from, each with their own unique features and appeal. Leave your worries and your clothes behind and take a dip in the mineral-rich waters surrounded by natural beauty at a traditional *onsen* like those at **Hakone Yuryo**, where travelers concerned about nudity in public hot springs that are separated by gender can also choose to book a private soak.

Speaking of warm waters, Hakone is an excellent place to attend a *chanoyu* (a guided ceremony led by a tea master) to learn about the rituals and etiquette of preparing and serving matcha. At **Hakuun-Do Tea Garden**, relax your mind and body in the lush greenery of **Hakone Gora Park**, as you're taught not just how to prepare and serve tea, but how to entertain guests and embrace Japanese customs of hospitality.

Depart Hakone rested and relaxed aboard a historic train on the **Hakone Tozan Railway**, one of Japan's most scenic train routes, winding through verdant mountains and charming villages with panoramic views of the Japanese countryside.

Above: *Japanese maples in fiery fall color in Hakone-Yumoto.*

KO SAMUI, THAILAND

Unwind to the sound of the waves lapping against the shore with a traditional Thai massage, an ancient healing therapy that combines acupressure, stretching, and rhythmic massage techniques to promote relaxation, relieve muscle tension, and improve circulation. **Dtu's Professional Massage** is one of the area's most popular options, featuring five-star reviews from thousands of happy customers across platforms.

Take a leisurely boat tour of Ko Samui's surrounding islands, **Ko Pha-Ngan** and **Ko Tao**, cruising through turquoise waters and stopping at secluded coves, snorkeling spots, and pristine beaches along the way.

Wander through lush tropical gardens like the **Secret Buddha Garden** or the **Samui Butterfly Garden**, where you can pass tranquil ponds and cascading waterfalls to discover exotic plants and rare wildlife species, immersing yourself in the Thai island's biodiversity and natural beauty.

Embark on a leisurely hike through verdant rainforests and jungle-clad mountains to popular waterfalls like **Na Muang Waterfall 1 and 2** or **Hin Lad Waterfall**, where you can cool off with a refreshing dip in the crystal-clear waters surrounded by tropical greenery.

Before your trip is over, don't miss your chance to take a class at organic farm-to-table Thai cooking school **Island Organics**. Unique to Ko Samui, the classes at Island Organics are some of the most detailed in Thailand, teaching students four traditional Thai recipes over the course of four hours, with produce picked fresh from their own farm, which cultivates more than 80 different types of fruits, vegetables, and herbs. You'll leave with a full belly and brain; and as a souvenir, the knowledge of how to prepare fresh coconut cream, curry pastes, refreshing herbal drinks, and more.

Right: *Thai-specialty snacks;*
Opposite: *Ang Thong Marine National Park, south of Ko Tao.*

PUGLIA, ITALY

When in Puglia, do as the Pugliesi do: go wine tasting in **Salento**, Puglia's southernmost region, where winemaking traditions and techniques have been passed down through generations. Smell, sip, swirl, and savor indigenous grape varieties like Primitivo, Negroamaro, and Malvasia from this sun-drenched *terroir* at wineries such as **Mottura** (get a bottle of the Villa Mottura), **Rosa del Golfo** (try the award-winning Rosato del Salento*)*, and **Antica Enotria** (don't hesitate to pick up the Sale della Terra).

Cycle through the UNESCO World Heritage Site of **Alberobello**, known for its distinctive *trulli* houses with their conical roofs. Admire the unique architecture of these traditional stone dwellings from the charming streets of the historic town center, accessed via scenic country lanes lined with olive trees and vineyards.

Or journey to another nearby UNESCO World Heritage Site, **Matera**, famous in **Basilicata** for its ancient cave dwellings and rock-cut churches. Wander through the labyrinthine streets of Matera's **Sassi** district to marvel at the frescoes and Byzantine artwork preserved within its ancient cave churches.

Board a boat to take a tour of the **Gargano Peninsula's** dramatic coastline to discover hidden sea caves and grottoes accessible only by boat, where you can swim, snorkel, and sunbathe in glassy waters. For more fun in the sun, enjoy a beach day at nearby **Polignano a Mare**, **Otranto**, or **Gallipoli**, where you can enjoy stunning views of the Adriatic or Ionian Sea, depending where you choose to park your sun bed.

Whatever you do, don't forget to set aside at least one evening in the 'White City' of **Ostuni**, a picturesque village of whitewashed streets adorned with bougainvillea-covered balconies. Perched atop a hill overlooking the Adriatic Sea, Ostuni is known to be home to the most beautiful sunsets in Puglia—maybe in all of Italy.

Left: Cone-roofed trulli *line the streets in the picturesque Puglian town of Alberobello, Italy.*

Seaside Sanctuaries

From Brighton Beach to the Balearic Sea and beyond, sandy shorelines and sea breezes await on the welcoming waterfronts in destinations around the world. Next stop: seaside serenity.

BOHOL, PHILIPPINES

Lush jungles and a laid-back atmosphere make Bohol—nestled in the **Central Visayas** region of the Philippines—an ideal destination for any traveler seeking a bit of coastal tranquility.

For a peaceful beach day, look no further than the pristine white sands of **Dumaluan Beach**, where calm, shallow waters are ideal for water activities. Snorkelers and divers will also want to make their way to **Balicasag Island** to see vibrant coral reefs teeming with tropical fish and sea turtles.

If you're more interested in finding the local party scene, nearby **Panglao Island** is the place to be. Perhaps the most popular shoreline in Bohol can be found here at **Alona Beach**, with powdery white sand that's ideal for sunbathing and crystal-clear waters for swimming—as well as beachfront beers at **Aluna Beach Lounge**, rooftop cocktails at **Salt & Sky**, karaoke at **Otso Otso Club**, and more.

For a different kind of adventure on the water, climb aboard a **Loboc River Cruise** to feast on delicious Filipino cuisine while being serenaded by local musicians demonstrating traditional songs and dances from around the Bohol region.

While you're almost certain to at least catch a *glimpse* of them during your travels, don't miss your chance to visit one of Bohol's most renowned natural wonders, the extraordinary **Chocolate Hills**. Climb to the top of a viewing point, such as the **Chocolate Hills Complex** in **Carmen**, for the most breathtaking view of this symbol of the region's unique geological heritage, a formation comprised of more than 1200 conical hills scattered across the Bohol landscape.

BRIGHTON, ENGLAND

The famous striped beach huts, pebbled shores, and views of the **English Channel** aren't all that make **Brighton Beach** such a popular seaside destination for queer travelers. It's not the nostalgic charm of the amusement park rides, arcades, and candy-floss stands at **Brighton Pier**, either.

If we're being honest, it's the proximity of all those classic summer scenes to the area's gay village of **Kemptown** that draws LGBTQ+ beachgoers back to Brighton year after year. From coffee shops and teahouses like **Cup of Joe** and **Metrodeco** to boozers **Blanch House Champagne and Cocktail Bar**, **Brighton Bier**, and **R-Bar**, laid-back Kemptown is Brighton's hub of queer culture, offering a picturesque respite for relaxation and rowdiness in equal measure to LGBTQ+ travelers seeking solace by the sea.

Nearby in the **Lanes**, visitors can wind through narrow alleyways and a maze of cobblestone streets to find a cornucopia of queer-friendly spots. Stop for a bite to eat at the aptly named and popular **Lost in the Lanes** cafe, shop sustainable fashion at **FAIR** and award-winning footwear at **Rieker**, or enjoy a drink or two at the **Flipside** before ending your evening with a cone of your favorite flavor at **Badiani Gelato**.

Just west of Brighton Pier you'll find **Hove Lawns**, a massive green space overlooking the sea that's ideal for picnics, kite flying, and leisurely strolls along the promenade. For even more of an adventure, you can rent a bike and cycle along the **Undercliff Walk**, which stretches from **Brighton Marina** to **Saltdean** with breathtaking views of the cliffs and coastline.

FLORIANÓPOLIS, BRAZIL

With over 40 different *praias* to choose from, beach-hopping is a must-do activity in Florianópolis. Start your day at **Praia de Campeche** to sunbathe on soft sands and go for leisurely swims in calm, transluscent waters. From there, go to **Praia da Joaquina**

Above: *Glide past palm trees and sample spectacular Filipino food on a Loboc River Cruise in Bohol, Philippines.*

in the afternoon for a beach with golden sand, otherworldly dunes, and world-class surfing conditions. Then end your day at **Praia Mole**, where you can watch the sunset over the cliffs along the coastline before heading to one of the area's many queer-friendly beach bars to kick off your evening in a lively atmosphere.

Those seeking more private waterfronts might prefer a trip to **Lagoinha do Leste**, a pristine, secluded beach between forested hills and coastline that's only accessible by boat or hiking trail. Or consider making your way to the sandy shores overlooking the Atlantic Ocean at **Barra da Lagoa**, where the calm waters at the mouth of a lagoon are ideal for swimming, kayaking, and paddleboarding.

Discover the tradition of oyster farming in **Santa Catarina**, where more than 90% of Brazil's oysters—and according to chefs, some of the world's best bivalves—come from. Visit a local farm like **Ostravagante Fazenda Marinha** to learn how the oysters are raised and, of course, to taste fresh Catarinense oysters harvested straight from the sea.

When you're not on the water or shucking oysters, tour local landmarks that tell the story of the city's heritage, such as the Portuguese-style architecture of the historic **Fortaleza de São José da Ponta Grossa**; the **Santo Antonio de Lisboa** district, with the Azorean culture and customs it has maintained since its 19th-century inception; and the **Hercílio Luz Bridge**, the longest suspension bridge in the country, which links the island of Santa Catarina to the mainland.

REHOBOTH BEACH, DELAWARE, USA

For a kitschy shore trip to remember, there's no better spot to spend your summer days on the East Coast than the eponymous Rehoboth Beach in the queer-friendly town of Rehoboth Beach, Delaware. Wide sandy shores offer plenty of space for sunbathing, and gentle waves invite swimmers and boogie-boarders alike to take a dip, but it's the

Right: Snorkel an underwater wonderland off Bohol, Philippines;
Opposite: *Fishing boats at Barra da Lagoa in Florianópolis, Brazil.*

buzzing **Rehoboth Beach Boardwalk** that makes this tiny beach town feel like something straight out of a nostalgic coming-of-age film set in the summertime.

No trip to the boardwalk would be complete without a visit to **Funland**, a small family-owned amusement park that's home to vintage carousel horses, family-friendly carnival games, and thrilling rides for all ages, such as the Super Flip and the Sea Dragon. Just be sure to get your cone of frozen custard from the famed **Kohr Brothers** *after* you've gone on all the rides, not before. And don't forget the rainbow sprinkles.

On nearby **1st St**, pair your pancake stacks with a side of sequins at **Goolee's Grille**, home to Rehoboth's original drag brunch, where host and local celebrity Ruby Sparkler welcomes a packed house the third Sunday of each month. Reservations are highly encouraged.

From there, it's an easy walk to **Rehoboth Art League (RAL)**, a nonprofit arts organization showcasing the work of hundreds of local artists, where you can discover paintings, sculptures, ceramics, and more creations reflecting the beauty and diversity of the region. If you're lucky, you might also be able to take a class or workshop with one of those local artists directly, depending what's on RAL's event calendar during your stay.

Outdoor enthusiasts can take to **Cape Henlopen State Park** for miles of pristine coastline along the Atlantic Ocean and the Delaware Bay, as well as sand dunes and nature trails perfect for hikers, bikers, and birders alike. For kayaking and paddleboarding along scenic waterways, look no further than **Rehoboth Bay**, where you can also expect to spot wildlife such as ospreys, herons, and dolphins as you glide through the creeks and marshes.

But for boating and fishing, not to mention spotting seabirds and dolphins, the best place in town is the **Indian River Inlet**. It's also where you'll find the most stunning sunsets over the water, so plan accordingly.

Left: *Dunes meet the Atlantic Ocean at Delaware's nature-rich Cape Henlopen State Park, USA.*

SITGES, SPAIN

With beaches galore, a legendary nightlife scene, and a history of LGBTQ+ acceptance dating back to the 1960s, Sitges has all the markings of an ideal seaside vacation for queer travelers. In the charming **Old Town**, the artistic **Maricel Museum** and the palatial **Palau de Maricel** are tucked away between narrow cobblestone streets along with the **Cau Ferrat Museum**, once the home and studio of Catalan artist Santiago Rusiñol, a notable member of the Modernisme movement that flourished in Sitges at the turn of the 20th century.

But let's be honest: most travelers are here for the beaches. Start in the heart of the city with one of the city's most popular ones, **Platja de la Fragata**, where you'll find golden sands, clear waters and, best of all, a bevy of *chiringuitos* (beach bars) to choose from along the shoreline; **Chiringuito Iguana** is a local favorite. Also just steps away from the town center, **Platja de la Ribera** is a family-friendly beach popular with visitors for its wide expanses of soft sand and beautiful views of the Mediterranean Sea, while **Platja de Sant Sebastià** sits over on the eastern end of Sitges with a picturesque shoreline and stunning views of the town's historic skyline.

While all of these beaches (and the other nine beaches in Sitges) are queer-friendly, it's **Platja de la Bassa Rodona** that stands out as the town's premier gay beach. It's typically packed with muscular men in small swimsuits, and is an easy walk to **Hotel Calipolis**, where the bulk of beachgoers set up their sun beds and umbrellas before retrieving their drinks and snacks of choice from nearby **Pic Nic**. The beach fills up with a lively crowd, so you'll want to get there early to snag a good spot.

If you're willing to make the approximately 30-minute trek to access it, you can find more peace and privacy at **Platja de l'Home Mort**, a nudist and gay-friendly beach that's off the beaten path in Sitges. Established in 1930, Platja de l'Home Mort is actually one of the world's first known gay beaches. Here, buffs in the buff trade sand for pebbles along a rocky shoreline, cruising in the privacy of the surrounding forests, and relaxing in hammocks to the sounds of waves crashing before making their way to **Casa Marc Beach Bar** for a glass of vino as the sun sets.

After dark, queer bars on all sides of the **Plaça Indústria** square and nearby **Joan Tarrida** pedestrian street beckon. Enjoy drinks on the terrace at **Parrots Pub**, drag shows at **Bitch Bar**, dancing at **Queenz**, or if you're feeling adventurous, fully naked parties every night at **Bourbons Bar**. *Salud* to that.

***Below:** Sitges' 17th-century Sant Bartomeu i Santa Tecla church;*
***Opposite:** Central Platja de Sant Sebastià, one of many beaches in and around Sitges.*

Trailblazing Travels

Trails don't discriminate; they welcome travelers from all walks of life with open arms, embracing and celebrating the diverse beauty of the natural world. From rugged coastlines to lush forests, here are some of the most stunning hiking trails in LGBTQ+-friendly countries around the world, for intermediate to advanced hikers.

BESSEGGEN RIDGE

....

LENGTH
14km (8.7 miles)

TIME
Six to eight hours

GETTING THERE
Just a four-hour drive (or a three-hour train ride) from Norway's Oslo Lufthavn Airport will bring you to **Gjendesheim**, a picturesque mountain lodge and the starting point for the Besseggen Ridge hike.

JOTUNHEIMEN, NORWAY

Located in the heart of the **Jotunheimen National Park**, the Besseggen Ridge hiking trail is steep and winding, and recommended for experienced hikers. Begin your journey from the **Gjendesheim** trailhead or take a boat cruise on the **Gjende Lake** from Gjendesheim to **Memurubu**, and start from there. Starting at Memurubu tends to be easier, since the route goes uphill.

Expect to encounter steep ascents and narrow ridges, as well as stunning views of two beautiful bodies of water, the distinctly emerald-hued Gjende Lake and the deep blue **Bessvatnet Lake**. From the highest point of the hike, the entire length of the ridge is visible, stretching out into the distance like a rugged spine cutting through the heart of Norway's untamed wilderness.

Above: *Hiking above Gjende and Bessvatnet Lakes on Jotunheimen's Besseggen Ridge Trail, Norway.*

NORTHERN SPAIN

The legendary Camino de Santiago pilgrimage—also known as the Way of St James—spans northern Spain and ultimately leads to the revered shrine of St James, the biblical apostle allegedly laid to rest in the **Catedral de Santiago de Compostela**.

Anyone who wishes to complete the Camino will need to get their **Credencial del Peregrino** (Pilgrim's Passport) from a local pilgrim office or church before they begin. These passports are stamped at designated locations along the trail and ultimately serve as proof of pilgrimage, granting participants access to pilgrim accommodations and to the **Compostela certificate** upon arrival in **Santiago de Compostela**.

Local residents in these regions, known as *hospitaleros*, typically provide food, lodging, and support to those completing the Camino, but you can also book overnight stays at *albergues* (pilgrim hostels) along the trail.

Along the **Camino Francés** route, between the Spanish towns of **Manjarín** and **Foncebadón**, is an iconic landmark called the **Cruz de Ferro**, a wooden pole about 1.5m (5ft) high, topped with an iron cross. Travelers completing the Camino are encouraged to bring along a stone from their homeland and leave it at the base of this cross, symbolically leaving their burdens behind before continuing their journey.

*Right: The Catedral de Santiago de Compostela—journey's end for pilgrims; **Opposite:** Setting out on the Way of St James' Camino Francés.*

CAMINO DE SANTIAGO

LENGTH
800km (497 miles)

TIME
About 30 days from start to finish

GETTING THERE
While visitors can embark upon the Camino de Santiago from various starting points throughout France, Portugal, and Spain, the best-known route—the **Camino Francés**—takes off from the foothills of the **Pyrenees Mountains** in the French town of **St-Jean Pied de Port**, then winds through the uniquely varied landscapes of the **Basque Country (Euskadi), Navarre, La Rioja, Castile and León, and Galicia**.

MACHU PICCHU, PERU

One of the world's most famous hiking routes and a UNESCO World Heritage Site, the **Inca Trail** in Peru spans from **Aguas Calientes** to the Sun Gate itself, **Intipunku**, overlooking the renowned ruins of Machu Picchu.

Permits are required to access the Inca Trail, and they often sell out months in advance, especially during peak season (from May to September), so it's important to secure them ahead of time through a licensed tour operator or travel agency.

The Inca Trail reaches dramatically high altitudes, with its highest point at more than 4200m (13,800ft) above sea level. To reduce the risk of altitude sickness, take time to acclimatize in **Cuzco**, the former capital of the Inca Empire, before beginning your trek. Consider exploring historic landmarks like **Plaza de Armas** and **Qorikancha** (Temple of the Sun) while acclimating to Andean altitudes.

This hiking route is not just a physical journey but a spiritual one, winding past sacred sites—the ruins of **Llactapata**, **Runkurakay**, **Sayaqmarka**, **Phuyupatamarka**, and **Wiñay Wayna**—and offering a window into the storied past of the Inca civilization.

From the highest point of the trail—**Warmiwañusca** (Dead Woman's Pass)—drink in panoramic views of the surrounding mountains and valleys. And of course, the ruins of Machu Picchu itself, with its ancient temples, terraces and plazas, serve as a breathtaking finale to the Inca Trail experience.

Opposite: *Market day in Cuzco, the ideal place to acclimatize before hiking the legendary Inca Trail.*

INCA TRAIL

....

LENGTH
43km (27 miles)

TIME
Four days and three nights

GETTING THERE
From **Cuzco**, Machu Picchu's closest airport, take the bus to **Ollantaytambo Station**, about a 1½-hour ride. From there, board the train to **Aguas Calientes Station** for another 1½-hour ride, bringing you to the starting point for your hike.

MT PICO

. . . .

LENGTH
7.1km (4.4 miles)

TIME
Eight hours

GETTING THERE
From the **Pico Airport**, it's about a 30-minute drive to the trail's start at **Casa da Montanha**.

Above: Tackle a tough out-and-back hike up the slopes of Mt Pico, Azores;
Opposite: Mountain views from Olympic National Park's Hurricane Ridge Visitor Center, USA.

AZORES, PORTUGAL

Set atop the rugged terrain of **Pico Island** in the Portuguese Azores, the volcanic crater at the summit of **Mt Pico** (known as **Pico Alto**) offers stunning views of the caldera and crater lake below—in part because, as the summit marker at Pico Alto will tell you, it's the highest point in all of Portugal at 2351m (7713ft).

The out-and-back trail is challenging, with both rough, rocky terrain and rapid weather changes at high altitudes.

Make reservations ahead of time, then check in at **Casa da Montanha** (Mountain House). You can take off in the morning to hike during the daytime or, for a truly unforgettable experience, opt to spend the night in Mt Pico's crater instead, embarking in the early evening and sleeping overnight in a tent before awaking to watch the sunrise from atop the third-highest mountain in the Atlantic.

WASHINGTON STATE, USA

For a choose-your-own-adventure hiking experience, look no further than the plethora of trails at **Olympic National Park** in Washington State. From short nature walks to backpacking routes spanning several days, you have approximately 982km (610 miles) of maintained trails to choose from. Local favorites are included below.

Hurricane Hill Trail

One of the most popular trails in the **Hurricane Ridge**, Hurricane Hill Trail climbs around 213m (699ft). While it's considered moderately strenuous, the panoramic views of the **Olympic Mountains**, the **Strait of Juan de Fuca**, and **Vancouver Island** make the effort expended more than worthwhile.

In late spring or early summer the Hurricane Hill Trail is adorned with vibrant, colorful wildflowers, such as lupine and avalanche lilies. This area is also home to a population of Olympic marmots, a unique species found only in the Olympic Mountains.

HURRICANE HILL TRAIL

LENGTH
5.5km (3.4 miles)

TIME
Two to three hours

GETTING THERE
The trailhead is at the end of **Hurricane Hill Rd**, about 3km (2 miles) past the **Hurricane Ridge Visitor Center**.

OZETTE LOOP

....

LENGTH
15.1km (9.4 miles)

TIME
Four to six hours

GETTING THERE
This starts and ends at **Cape Alava**, the westernmost point of the continental United States.

Ozette Loop

The Ozette Loop offers a particularly unique hiking experience, thanks to several sections of elevated cedar boardwalks traversing through dense coastal forests and wetlands, designed to protect the area's fragile ecosystems from being trampled.

In the four to six hours it typically takes to complete this hike, travelers can explore tide pools teeming with marine life and enjoy sweeping views of the Pacific Ocean. About halfway through the loop, hikers will reach **Sand Point**, a scenic beach that makes an excellent spot for picnicking, beachcombing, and watching for passing whales or seals.

Above: *Coastal scenery along the Ozette Loop;*
Opposite: *A cool-down dip after hiking the Olympic National Park trails.*

Hoh River Trail

The Hoh River Trail hike can be completed as a day trip for the ambitious, or a multiday backpacking excursion. Permits are required in advance, and be prepared for rain and fog, as well as muddy and slippery sections throughout the trail.

As its name implies, this trail follows the scenic **Hoh River**, offering opportunities for fishing and waterfront picnics. A short side-trail here, known as the **Hall of Mosses**, leads to a magical grove of old-growth trees draped in lush green moss, offering a glimpse into the enchanting beauty of the **Hoh Rainforest**. Experienced backpackers can also access the **Blue Glacier** from this trail, a spectacular, almost otherworldly icy blue landmark located high in the Olympic Mountains.

HOH RIVER TRAIL

....

LENGTH
28km (17.4 miles)

TIME
Two to four days

GETTING THERE
The trail begins just next to the **Hoh Rainforest Visitor Center**.

The Future of LGBTQ+ Travel

I'd be remiss not to acknowledge the barriers that still persist within the tourism industry for queer travelers. Despite the progress we've made, *many* LGBTQ+ travelers—not to mention BIPOC travelers, disabled travelers, and more—continue to face discrimination and limited access to safe and welcoming spaces while traveling, whether abroad or in their own home countries.

On the one hand, hotels, tourism boards, airlines, and other businesses in the travel industry are responsible for doing more to remove these obstacles. They need to commit to inclusivity, offer comprehensive training for their staff, and actively promote safe spaces for all travelers, regardless of their sexual orientation or gender identity.

"Do I wish I still had to do LGBTQ+ sensitivity training with companies 30 years into my career? No, I hoped my work here would be done by now," said **Ed Salvato**, author of *Handbook of LGBT Tourism and Hospitality: A Guide for Business Practice* and longtime leader in LGBTQ+ hospitality training. "The community has changed a great deal in the past three decades that I've been in this business, but there's still plenty of work to do."

On the other hand, there's also an onus on travel bloggers and other content creators to recommend responsibly—and transparently—when publishing content targeted toward LGBTQ+ travelers.

"The double-edged sword, which I think is just, unfortunately, an internet phenomenon, is that usually traveler influencers aren't going places of their own accord. They're not picking something off the map and showing up," said **Yasmin Benoit**, an award-winning asexual activist, writer, public speaker, and one of the UK's most prominent Black alternative models. "Usually there's some type of arrangement going on, maybe with the hotel or some other aspect of the tourism industry, which would lead them there. Not necessarily to say 'this is an advertisement,' but maybe to make their experience different. Because they'll be in the nicest spots, the best hotels, and they'll be treated in a certain way that isn't necessarily how you'd be treated as any other tourist visiting that destination."

Yasmin and I agreed that the content these creators post during these agreed-upon trips needs to be more honest and thorough in the interest of LGBTQ+ travelers' safety.

"The part that seems to get lost in translation is all the stuff that's going on in between the highlight reels. No one's posting, 'Oh, I got stranded after the airport and I couldn't get to that spot, so I had to do all of this,' or 'I wouldn't have felt safe hanging around in this area by myself waiting for this thing to come,'" Yasmin said. "There are so many components of travel that can play a part in determining if you want to visit a place or not that people don't have time to get into in an Instagram post or a video on TikTok, and people aren't writing those giant blog posts about things as much anymore because people's attention spans are too short. So, it's much harder to get the full story nowadays."

Yasmin also pointed out that, more often than not, these opportunities and travel arrangements tend to be offered only to content creators that fit a certain profile.

"It tends to be younger, white, thin, cis male gays," she explained. "So then even though I might think 'Oh, that place does look really cool,' when they post about wherever they are, it might not be cool for *me*—because if I don't fit that same description, then it might not be safe for me as a person of color or someone femme-presenting."

Ed said he's seen the same thing time and again throughout his three decades in the industry.

"I think it's gay white males that have the most privilege and have benefited the most from all of the progress the community has made," Ed said. "And because that group is the most visible, we're the ones that are marketed to, and then it becomes very chicken-and-egg. Like, 'Well, we got a lot of money from the gay white men, so we'll keep marketing to the gay white men.' But that's what we need to espouse. We need to consider the needs of communities of color and be much more intersectional to include them. And we need more understanding about the letters beyond the G and the L in the acronym, too."

From both ends of the LGBTQ+ travel spectrum—from the businesses in the industry to the content creators they're hosting—we deserve better. But what does that look like?

From the perspective of the businesses, Ed literally wrote the book on inclusivity in the tourism industry, and he continues to lead hospitality courses for staff at companies who want to get it right.

"We're trying to get employees to strip away assumptions and look at the person in front of them as an individual," Ed says. Whatever biased thoughts you might have about this person, throw them out the window. Be in a position of openness. Focus on trying to understand the people in front of you. Welcome them, introduce yourself, let them introduce themself, ask how you can help them, then help them like you'd help any other guest. It's so much less hard than people expect it to be, and it makes so much more of a difference than they think it will."

The founder of the UK-based queer travel organization Moonlight Experiences, **Aisha**

Shaibu-Lenoir has found that when places work to accommodate underserved communities, it often ends up benefiting the majority, too.

"A lot of things the LGBTQ+ community does, end up supporting all people," Aisha explained. "For example, if we have trans rights, then Black people can feel safer in spaces, which then means it's likely that women will feel safer in those spaces, too. White women, gay men, everyone will feel safer in those spaces because there's this ripple effect, which I think a lot of straight people don't recognize because they already have that privilege. Often there is this hierarchy and inequality. So, a lot of the time, we're doing the work to try to level the playing field for people who maybe don't have those privileges."

Despite the additional challenges our community faces, after the year I've spent interviewing queer travelers from welcoming destinations around the world for this book, I truly believe that the future looks bright for the LGBTQ+ travel community.

More places around the world continue to embrace inclusivity and diversity. Just in the time I've been working on this book, India struck down the anti-trans Telangana Eunuchs Act of 1919; China's top court in Hong Kong ruled in favor of legally recognizing same-sex partnerships; the prime minister of Andorra came out as the country's first openly gay head of government; and Thailand legalized same-sex marriage. Step by painstaking step, the world is gradually becoming a more inviting place for LGBTQ+ adventurers to explore safely.

The growing visibility and acceptance of LGBTQ+ travelers signals a shift toward a more equitable travel experience for all. With each journey, each step forward, we witness the unique power of travel to bridge divides, foster understanding, and build a more intersectional-inclusive world. Our collective future as LGBTQ+ travelers holds promise. It holds hope.

So, let's continue to advocate for change, working toward a world where *every* journey is not just safe but enriching and empowering for *every* traveler. But let's also celebrate the progress we've made. Let's cherish the connections we've forged through our travels and continue to build even more of them as we're able. Together, we can create a future where the freedom to explore knows no bounds and where the spirit of adventure is accessible to everyone.

"Go out into the world and discover a little bit of the queer culture in other countries. It will make you feel more connected to the world. You'll see that you're not alone—you're a part of this great fabric, woven into the tapestry of LGBTQ+ explorers throughout history," Ed said. "The radical act of traveling while queer will reconnect you with a different part of yourself, and it will connect you with a different kind of family. And that's a beautiful thing."

LGBTQ+ TRAVEL ESSENTIALS

Know Your Rights

Equaldex

equaldex.com

Up-to-date status and timelines of LGBTQ+ rights in each country, state, province, and region around the world, including the legal status of same-sex marriage, adoption, serving openly in the military, discrimination protections, age of consent differences, blood-donation restrictions, gender-changing restrictions, and gay-conversion-therapy bans.

ILGA World Maps

ilga.org/ilga-world-maps

Interactive and constantly updated visual representations of how LGBTIQ people are affected by laws and policies around the world. These maps cover more than 100 topics, including sexual orientation, gender identity and expression, and sex characteristics (SOGIESC) globally; as well as how those issues are addressed in international human rights mechanisms like the Universal Periodic Review, Treaty Bodies, or Special Procedures within the United Nations.

Rights for Trans Travelers

transequality.org/resources/know-your-rights-airport-security

The National Center for Transgender Equality answer common questions trans people may have about airport security procedures, and outline steps individuals can take to prevent and respond to problems at the airport.

Practical Safety Tips

IGLTA LGBTQ+ Safety Guide

iglta.org/destinations/travel-guides/lgbtq-safety-guide

A comprehensive guide to LGBTQ+ travel safety from the International LGBTQ+ Travel Association in partnership with Destination Pride.

Information for LGBTQI+ Travelers

travel.state.gov/content/travel/en/international-travel/before -you-go/travelers-with-special-considerations/lgbtqi.html

International travel recommendations for travelers with special considerations, specifically LGBTQI+ travelers, from the US Department of State Bureau of Consular Affairs.

LGBTQ+ Foreign Travel Advice

gov.uk/guidance/lesbian-gay-bisexual-and-transgender -foreign-travel-advice

Foreign, Commonwealth & Development Office (FCDO) advice for lesbian, gay, bisexual, and transgender (LGBTQ+) people traveling abroad from the UK.

In Case of Emergency

Rainbow Railroad

rainbowrailroad.org/request-help

A global not-for-profit organization that helps at-risk LGBTQI+ people get to safety worldwide through emergency relocation, crisis response, cash assistance, and other forms of assistance.

SAGE LGBTQ+ Elder Hotline

1-877-360-LGBT [5428]

Confidential support and crisis response available 24/7 in English and Spanish, with translation in 180 languages, through Services and Advocacy for LGBTQ+ Elders (SAGE).

The Trevor Project

thetrevorproject.org/get-help

Crisis intervention services for LGBTQ+ people under age 25, available 24 hours a day, 7 days a week, 365 days a year. Text START to 678678, call 1-866-488-7386, or visit the website.

Trans Lifeline

translifeline.org/hotline

A grassroots hotline and micro-grants 501(c)(3) nonprofit organization offering direct emotional and financial support to trans people in crisis. Call 1-877-656-8860 or visit the website.

ADDITIONAL LGBTQ+ TRAVEL RESOURCES

Worldwide Pride Calendar

One of the main missions of this book is to emphasize that LGBTQ+ travelers deserve every opportunity to travel to inclusive spaces around the world *outside* of just Pride festivals. That being said, some LGBTQ+ travelers do love the idea of traveling specifically to take part in Pride parades, protests, and more—and it can be tough to know precisely where and when to find these festivities.

Luckily, Pride isn't confined to the month of June. Different countries and regions host their own unique Pride celebrations at all sorts of different times throughout the year.

JANUARY

Cologne, Germany: LGBT Carnival
Melbourne, Victoria, Australia: Midsumma Festival
Reykjavík, Iceland: Rainbow Reykjavík
Yangon, Myanmar: Yangon Pride Festival &PROUD LGBTIQ Film Festival

FEBRUARY

Ahmedabad, India: Ahmedabad Queer Pride
Auckland, New Zealand/Aotearoa: Auckland Pride Festival
Cape Town, South Africa: Cape Town Pride
Kathmandu, Nepal: Mitini Nepal Pride Parade
Melbourne, Victoria, Australia: Midsumma Pride March
Miami, Florida, USA: Gay8 Festival
Sydney, New South Wales, Australia: Mardi Gras LGBTQI+ Festival

MARCH

Cape Coral, Florida, USA: Pride Cape Coral
Kathmandu, Nepal: Queer Womxn Pride
Metz, France: Gay Pride Lorraine
Palm Springs, California, USA: White Party Palm Springs
Phuket, Thailand: Phuket Pride
Tampa, Florida, USA: Tampa Pride
Wellington, New Zealand/Aotearoa: Wellington Pride Festival

APRIL

Jasper, Alberta, Canada: Jasper Pride Festival
Miami Beach, Florida, USA: Miami Beach Pride
Nice, France: In&Out
Philadelphia, Pennsylvania, USA: Philly Black Pride
Phoenix, Arizona, USA: Phoenix Pride
Tokyo, Japan: Tokyo Rainbow Pride

MAY

Beirut, Lebanon: Beirut Pride
Bhopal, India: Bhopal Pride March
Birmingham, England: Birmingham Pride
Bratislava, Slovakia: Dúhový Pride
Brussels, Belgium: Belgian Pride
Bucharest, Romania: Bucharest Pride
Caracas, Venezuela: Caracas Pride
Chiang Mai, Thailand: Chiang Mai Pride
Maspalomas, Gran Canaria, Spain: Pride Maspalomas
Ghent, Belgium: Queer Pride Ghent
Gugulethu, Western Cape, South Africa: Khumbulani Pride
Long Beach, California, USA: Long Beach Pride Parade & Festival
Moscow, Russia: Moscow Pride
Nicosia, Cyprus: Cyprus Pride
Northampton, Massachusetts, USA: Noho Pride
Orlando, Florida, USA: Orlando Black Pride
Puerto Vallarta, Mexico: Vallarta Pride
Rīga, Latvia: Baltic Pride
Springfield, Illinois, USA: Springfield PrideFest
Torremolinos, Spain: Torremolinos Pride
Vienna, Austria: Vienna Pride
Vilnius, Lithuania: Baltic Pride
Warsaw, Poland: Equality Parade

JUNE

Annapolis, Maryland, USA: Annapolis Pride Parade & Festival
Athens, Greece: Athens Pride
Austin, Texas, USA: Austin Pride Parade
Bangkok, Thailand: Bangkok Pride
Bengaluru (Bangalore), India: Bengaluru Pride
Binghamton, New York, USA: Pride Palooza
Bristol, England: Bristol Pride
Budapest, Hungary: Budapest Pride
Chicago, Illinois, USA: Chicago Pride Fest

Columbus, Ohio, USA: Stonewall Columbus
Denver, Colorado, USA: Denver PrideFest
Dublin, Ireland: Dublin Pride
Gothenburg, Sweden: West Pride Gothenburg
Helsinki, Finland: Helsinki Pride
Iowa City, Iowa, USA: Iowa City Pride
İstanbul, Türkiye: Lambda İstanbul Pride Week
Kathmandu, Nepal: Nepal Pride Parade
Key West, Florida, USA: Key West Pride
Kolkata (Calcutta), India: Kolkata Rainbow Pride Walk
Lisbon, Portugal: Lisbon LGBT Pride Parade
London, England: Pride in London
Los Angeles, California, USA: LA Pride
Madrid, Spain: Madrid Pride
Manila, Philippines: Metro Manila Pride
Memphis, Tennessee, USA: Tri-State Black Pride
Mexico City, Mexico: Mexico City Pride
Middletown, Connecticut, USA: Middletown Pride
Milan, Italy: Milano Pride
Minneapolis, Minnesota, USA: Twin Cities Pride
Munich, Germany: Munich Pride
Nashville, Tennessee, USA: Nashville Pride
Oklahoma City, Oklahoma, USA: Oklahoma City Pride
Orlando, Florida, USA: One Magical Weekend
Oslo, Norway: Oslo Pride
Pattaya, Thailand: Circuit Festival Asia
Pittsburgh, Pennsylvania, USA: Pittsburgh Pride
Provincetown, Massachusetts, USA: Provincetown Pride
Raleigh, North Carolina, USA: Raleigh Pride
Rome, Italy: Roma Pride
San Francisco, California, USA: San Francisco Pride
San Juan, Puerto Rico: Pride Puerto Rico

São Paulo, Brazil: São Paulo Pride
Seattle, Washington, USA: Seattle Pride
Shanghai, China: Shanghai Pride
Sitges, Spain: Sitges Pride
Skopje, North Macedonia: Skopje Pride
Sofia, Bulgaria: Sofia Pride
Split, Croatia: Split Pride
Tbilisi, Georgia: Tbilisi Pride
Tel Aviv, Israel: Tel Aviv Pride Parade
Toronto, Ontario, Canada: Pride Toronto
West Hollywood, California, USA: WeHo Pride
Zürich, Switzerland: Zürich Pride Festival

JULY

Amsterdam, Netherlands: Pride Amsterdam
Barcelona, Spain: Pride Barcelona
Berlin, Germany: Berlin Pride
Cologne, Germany: ColognePride
Dublin, Ireland: Trans & Intersex Pride
Esch-sur-Alzette, Luxembourg: Luxembourg Pride
Geneva, Switzerland: Geneva Pride
Limerick, Ireland: Limerick Pride
Ljubljana, Slovenia: Ljubljana Pride
London, Ontario, Canada: Pride London Festival
Marseille, France: Pride Marseille
Philadelphia, Pennsylvania, USA: Philadelphia Pride March & Festival
Porto, Portugal: Porto Pride Parade
San Diego, California, USA: San Diego Pride
Stockholm, Sweden: Stockholm Pride
Stuttgart, Germany: Stuttgart Pride Parade
Tórshavn, Faroe Islands: Faroe Pride

AUGUST

Antwerp, Belgium: Antwerp Pride
Azores Islands, Portugal: Pride Azores
Belfast, Northern Ireland: Belfast Pride

Brighton, England: Brighton & Hove Pride
Charlotte, North Carolina, USA:
Charlotte Pride
Copenhagen, Denmark: Copenhagen Pride
Frankfurt, Germany: Frankfurt Pride
Hamburg, Germany: Hamburg Pride
London, England: UK Black Pride
Manchester, England: Manchester Pride
Mariehamn, Åland, Finland: Åland Pride
Montréal, Quebec, Canada: Montréal Pride
Nottingham, England: Notts Pride
Prague, Czechia: Prague Pride
Reykjavík, Iceland: Reykjavík Pride
Tallinn, Estonia: Tallinn Pride

SEPTEMBER

Asheville, North Carolina, USA: Blue
Ridge Pride
Lexington, Kentucky, USA: Kentucky Black
Pride Festival
Osijek, Croatia: Osijek Pride
Rotterdam, Netherlands: Rotterdam Pride
Sarajevo, Bosnia & Hercegovina: Bosnian-
Herzegovinian (BiH) Pride March
Soweto, South Africa: Soweto Pride
Valletta, Malta: Malta Pride

OCTOBER

Atlanta, Georgia, USA: Atlanta Pride
Banff, Alberta, Canada: Banff Pride
Belgrade, Serbia: Belgrade Pride
Gaborone, Botswana: Gaborone Pride
Johannesburg, South Africa:
Johannesburg Pride
Las Vegas, Nevada, USA: Las Vegas Pride
Minsk, Belarus: Minsk Gay Pride
Palm Springs, California, USA: Greater Palm
Springs Pride
Phoenix, Arizona, USA: Phoenix Pride
Podgorica, Montenegro: Montenegro Pride

Tulsa, Oklahoma, USA: Tulsa Pride

NOVEMBER

Buenos Aires, Argentina: Buenos Aires Pride
Goa, India: Pride de Goa
Hong Kong, China: Hong Kong Pride Parade
Liverpool, England: Homotopia
Maspalomas, Gran Canaria, Spain:
Maspalomas Winter Pride
Palm Springs, California, USA: Palm
Springs Pride
Pattaya, Thailand: Pattaya Gay Festival
Santiago, Chile: Gay Parade Chile

DECEMBER

Reykjavík, Iceland: Pink December

LGBTQ+ Travel Agencies, Tours, Publications & Apps

LGBTQ+ TRAVEL AGENCIES & TOUR COMPANIES

Atlantis Events

atlantisevents.com

West Hollywood, California, USA

Largest gay and lesbian travel company in the world, offering cruises and resort vacations.

Concierge Travel

conciergetravel.cc

Houston, Texas, USA

Offers LGBTQ+ group travel, cruises, and customized travel-planning services.

Detours Travel

detourstravel.com

Vancouver, British Columbia, Canada

Provides group trips for gay travelers to destinations like Thailand, Greece, Costa Rica, and Spain.

HE Travel

hetravel.com

Salt Lake City, Utah, USA

Offers an extensive range of tours on every continent, catering to all members of the LGBTQIA+ community, with a focus on cultural and environmentally friendly travel.

Olivia Travel

olivia.com

San Francisco, California, USA

Offers cruises, resorts, and adventure travel exclusively for lesbians and queer women.

Oscar Wilde Tours

oscarwildetours.com

New York City, New York, USA

Founded by a gay history scholar. Offers historical LGBTQ+ tours in such cities as New York, London, Amsterdam, and Berlin.

OUT Adventures

outadventures.com

Toronto, Ontario, Canada

Provides exclusive cruises, tours, and themed adventures to destinations including Nepal, Antarctica, Kenya, and Vietnam.

Out in the Vineyard

outinthevineyard.com

Sonoma, California, USA

Specializes in LGBTQ+ wine-country tours and events in Sonoma and Napa Valleys.

Out Of Office

outofoffice.com

London, England

Specializes in luxury LGBTQ+ travel, including honeymoons and tailor-made trips.

OUTstanding Travel

outstandingtravel.com

Tel Aviv, Israel

Specializes in gay Mediterranean travel, offering trips to Israel, Greece, Jordan, Italy, Egypt, and Spain.

Pink Iceland

pinkiceland.is

Reykjavík, Iceland

Specializes in day tours, weddings, events, and tailor-made luxury travel for LGBTQ+ visitors to Iceland.

Pride Travelers

pridetravelers.com

US-wide

Gay-owned and operated, offering customizable travel experiences with exclusive deals and promotions.

Purple Light Vacations

purplelightvacations.com

San Diego, California, USA

Offers customized service for LGBTQ+ travelers, including all-inclusive gay vacations and cruises, as well as mainstream options.

Purple Roofs

purpleroofs.com

US-wide

Directory of LGBTQ+-owned and LGBTQ+-friendly lodging, travel agents, and tour operators worldwide.

Quiiky Travel

quiiky.com

Milan, Italy

Italy's first LGBTQ+ tour operator, offering customized trips and guided tours with an LGBTQ+ focus.

R Family Vacations

rfamilyvacations.com

New York, New York, USA

Offers LGBTQ+ family-friendly trips and adults-only vacations on land and at sea.

Rainbow Getaways

rainbowgetaways.net

Florida, USA

Provides tailor-made vacations for the LGBTQIA+ community, including family and group travel.

Source Journeys

sourceevents.com

Miami, Florida, USA

Organizes all-gay charters, and private LGBTQ+ groups aboard larger cruise ships, personalized cruise journeys, and group itineraries.

Toto Tours

tototours.com

Chicago, Illinois, USA

Specializes in adventure tours for LGBTQ+ travelers, focusing on unique and off-the-beaten-path destinations.

VACAYA

myvacaya.com

New York, New York, USA

LGBTQ+ getaways on chartered cruise ships and to all-LGBTQ+ international resorts.

Venture Out

venture-out.com

San Francisco, California, USA

Offers small-group cultural, historical, and nature tours to such destinations as Spain, Italy, Malta, Scotland, Southern Africa, and Japan.

Venture Out Project

ventureoutproject.com

Massachusetts, USA

Organizes LGBTQ+-specific backpacking trips in the US for teens, adults, and families, promoting outdoor education and inclusion.

Voyemo

voyemo.com

Berlin, Germany

Specializes in luxury travel, custom-made trips, and LGBTQ+-friendly destinations worldwide.

Zoom Vacations

zoomvacations.com

Chicago, Illinois, USA

Provides luxury LGBTQ+ group-travel packages and custom private tours worldwide.

LGBTQ+ TRAVEL PUBLICATIONS

Attitude Magazine

attitude.co.uk

London, England

Magazine offering travel features, lifestyle content, and news for gay men.

Curve Magazine

curvemag.com

San Francisco, California, USA

Magazine focusing on travel, entertainment, news, and lifestyle for lesbian and queer women.

Diva Magazine

divamag.co.uk

London, England

Magazine offering travel tips, lifestyle features, and news for lesbian and bisexual women.

Everyqueer

everyqueer.com

New York, New York, USA

Detailed travel guides, curated lesbian events, and worldwide LGBTQ+ tours teaching queer travelers how to safely see the world.

Gay Star News

gaystarnews.co.uk

London, England

News and travel website offering LGBTQ+ travel news, guides, and destination information.

Gay Times

gaytimes.co.uk

London, England

Magazine offering travel features, news, and lifestyle content for LGBTQ+ readers.

GayCities

gaycities.com

San Francisco, California, USA

Online travel guide recommending gay-friendly bars, clubs, restaurants, hotels, and more in 238 different cities globally.

GlobalGayz

globalgayz.com

Worldwide

Online travel blog providing LGBTQ+ news, stories, and travel tips.

Lonely Planet's LGBTQ+ Travel Guides

www.lonelyplanet.com/news/category/lgbtqia

Worldwide

Travel guides and resources specifically curated for LGBTQ+ travelers.

Out Traveler

outtraveler.com

New York, New York, USA

Destination guides, traveler advice, and coverage of top travel destinations and experiences for LGBTQ+ travelers.

Passport Magazine

passportmagazine.com

New York, New York, USA

Travel magazine providing LGBTQ+ travelers with news, travel advice, and destination info.

Queer in the World

queerintheworld.com

Worldwide

Travel blog offering guides, travel tips, and information on LGBTQ+-friendly destinations.

Travel Gay

travelgay.com

London, England

Serves a predominantly gay male audience with city guides, hotel recommendations, and event listings.

Two Bad Tourists

twobadtourists.com

Madrid, Spain

Travel blog by a gay couple providing travel tips, city guides, and LGBTQ+-friendly info.

Utopia Asia

utopia-asia.com

Bangkok, Thailand

Travel resource providing LGBTQ+ guides and news for destinations in Asia.

World Rainbow Hotels

worldrainbowhotels.com

New York, New York, USA

Directory of stylish, queer-friendly hotels in LGBTQ+-friendly destinations worldwide.

LGBTQ+ TRAVEL APPS

Everywhere Is Queer

everywhereisqueer.com

Map app featuring LGBTQIA+-owned spaces and businesses in locations all over the world.

Gaydar

gaydar.net

Dating app for gay and bisexual men, featuring travel options and city guides.

GayOut

gayout.com

App offering event listings, travel guides, and destination information for LGBTQ+ travelers.

Grindr

grindr.com

Social-networking app for gay, bi, trans, and queer people, offering travel features and local events.

HER

weareher.com

Dating and social-networking app for LGBTQ+ women, featuring travel communities and events.

Hornet

hornet.com

Social-networking app for gay men that also offers travel guides and destination information.

Meetup

meetup.com/topics/lgbt-travel

App connecting LGBTQ+ travelers to find travel buddies and join local LGBTQ+ travel groups.

Misterb&b

misterbandb.com

Accommodation app offering LGBTQ+-friendly places to stay, similar to Airbnb but for the LGBTQ+ community.

SCRUFF

scruff.com

Dating and social-networking app for gay, bi, trans, and queer men, also offering travel features and city guides.

Spartacus

spartacus.gayguide.travel

Travel app providing detailed gay guides to cities, including bars, clubs, saunas, and events.

Taimi

taimi.com

Social-networking and dating app for LGBTQ+ people, offering travel communities and destination tips.

Travel Gay

travelgay.com/mobile-app

Mobile app offering gay city guides, hotel recommendations, and event listings.

Index

Acknowledgments

Writing this book has been a deeply personal and transformative experience. It has reinforced my belief in the power of travel to open minds, foster connections, and promote inclusivity; and I've been so fortunate to be surrounded by a community of passionate, dedicated, and inspiring people who share my vision for a world where every traveler can explore freely and safely.

I find myself overwhelmed but, for once, it's not with all the tasks on my to-do list—it's with gratitude for the incredible support and encouragement I've received over the past year.

To Maria Ribas, without whom this book quite literally would not exist: thank you for the pivotal role you played in bringing this project to life, your unwavering belief in me as an author, the dozens of hours-long Zoom calls we've had together in the past year, your soothing responses to my frantic middle-of-the-night emails and text messages, and the endless gift of your friendship. If I could give you the shared dream house we mentally designed together while drinking wine on the terrace around the corner from my apartment in Amsterdam, I would. For now, I'll send *stroopwafel*.

To Becca Hunt, Emily Dubin, Karyn Noble, and the rest of the team at Lonely Planet that worked with me to get this book out into the world: thank you for believing in my vision and concept, investing in this resource for the LGBTQ+ travel community, guiding me through the publishing process for the first time as a debut author, working with me to make this book as useful and beautiful as possible, and not making fun of my Google Drive organization preferences or my obsession with the em dash. I will be forever grateful for this opportunity to fulfill my lifelong dream of becoming a published travel author—and for *Lonely fucking Planet*, no less! What a gift!

To every wonderful person I had the good fortune to interview for this book: Aisha Shaibu-Lenoir, Aurelia St Clair, Auston Matta, Barb Snelgrove, Charlie Sprinkman, Charly Stoever, Clovis Casemiro, Daan Colijn, Daniel DeFranco, Daniele Catena, David Brown, Diana Laskaris, Ed Salvato, Justine Goldon, Karl Krause, Lauren Aadland, Lexie Shaibu-Lenoir, Lisa Halling-Aadland, Luigi Cocciolo, Mairi Oliver, Melinda Murillo, Mina Jack Tolu, Paige Poprocky, Pan Pan Narkprasert, Regennia Johnson, Sam Goldon, Sam Slupski, Sue Reddel, Yasmin Benoit, and Yoliswa Moleboheng Mqoco. I can't thank you enough for being a part of this project. Your contributions are going to help so many queer travelers see your corners of the world safely and joyfully.

To my parents, Jenny and Dave Cassell: for instilling in me from a young age the idea that I can do anything I put my mind to if I work hard, trust my gut, and follow my heart.

To my nana, Alice Wanner: for my name, my genes, and the advice she's given me time and again for as long as I can remember: "Don't take no shit."

To my pap, Earl Stan Wanner: who was certain I'd do big things one day long before I let myself believe it, too. I hope you'd be proud of me for this—oh boy, oh boy, oh boy.

To my brother, Derrek Thomas: for barely batting an eye when I came out to him as bi, teaching me very early in life the importance of having thick skin, and along with my sweet sister-in-law, Jordan Collier, giving me my precious niece Emma James.

To the rest of my family: the whole rowdy bunch of aunts and uncles and cousins, for supporting me even when they may not totally understand me. I'm incredibly lucky to be related to you. Well, related to most of you. Some of you just kind of showed up one day and we kept you. I'm lucky to have you in my life, too.

To my best friends and chosen family: where would I be without you? Thank you to my oldest friend, Abby Akers, who has referred to herself as the Gayle to my Oprah for going on two decades now; to Anna Somers and Katie Blitz for being my constant cheerleaders throughout this and every other endeavor I've taken on in the last 10 years; to Whitney Schwalm for being my on-call emotional support human; to Mel Fox for encouraging me to be myself loudly and proudly; to Ali Greenberg for sharing her Drag Bingo winnings with me and introducing me to *RuPaul's Drag Race*; to Victoria Newlon for setting aside time to watch *Drag Race* 'together' every week from our respective continents; to Bethany Silva and her husband, Travis Miller, who make watching *Drag Race* each week possible; to Carly Romeo for encouraging me as I neared the finish line of this manuscript, and for that time she invited me to stay at Gloria Steinem's place in New York with her; to Haley Weaver for making me feel less alone as a fellow anxious author and defector from the marketing agency that shall not be named; to MaryClaire and Julien Guh for their endless positivity; to Bryan Buttigieg and Nick DeLuna for accepting me as one of their own despite not being from Long Island; to the Groffs for welcoming me with open arms and treating me like a part of their family without a second thought; and to all the other friends I'm sure I'm forgetting because AuDHD makes things fall out of my brain sometimes and also because writing all of this out is making me emotional, so I might need to step away to cry happy tears for a little while.

To our sweet and scrappy Stella, and in memory of our good girl Luna: for every ounce of love and comfort they've been kind and generous enough to give us over the years. We don't deserve dogs, honestly, but I'm so grateful they deal with us anyway.

To the love of my life, Andrew Valenski: for everything. I love you and I like you. After all this time. Always. Same team.

To every single reader who picks up this book: from the bottom of my heart, thank you. I'm honored that you're here and humbled to have your attention when there are so many things vying for it. So, sincerely, thank you. And I do mean you. Yes, you. *Thank you.*

PHOTO CREDITS

Front Cover: (clockwise from top left) Meegan Mitchell; Alexanderstock23/Shutterstock; Couple of Men; T Atkins/ Grexsys, LLC/500px; Stijn Nieuwendijk; Leticia Souza Photography; Pangina Heals; Mikhail Sotnikov/Getty Images; Gayly Planet / **Back Cover** (clockwise from top left) Travelpix Ltd/Getty Images; Sam Vargas Photography via Dunes Resort; Mistervlad/Adobe Stock; Nataliya Hora/Shutterstock; Gunter Nuyts/Shutterstock; Jordan Siemens/Getty Images; Johner Images/Getty Images / **6:** Paula Akpan / **9:** Alicia Valenski / **14:** Lauren Mulligan for Lonely Planet; Meegan Mitchell / **15:** spooh/ Getty Images / **16:** Gary Latham for Lonely Planet / **16–17:** Gunter Nuyts/Shutterstock / **18:** David Ross, via Pardus Fine Art / **19:** Finn stock/Shutterstock / **20:** Austin Bush for Lonely Planet / **21:** Pangina Heals / **22:** AsiaDreamPhoto/Alamy / **23:** Richard I'Anson for Lonely Planet / **24:** Beef.Bkk / **25:** Eat Me Restaurant / **26–27:** Carlos Nizam/Getty Images / **28:** Goncharovaia/Shutterstock; Couple of Men / **29:** Wut_Moppie/ Shutterstock / **30–31:** Davide Giauna, via Prik; Stijn Nieuwendijk / **32:** Marilène Zeeman/SAILORSCAMERA, via Club NYX / **33:** Anton_Ivanov/Shutterstock / **34:** Chris Mueller/Getty Images / **35:** Mairi Oliver, via Lighthouse Books / **36–37:** Guven Ozdemir/ Getty Images / **37:** Robert Ormerod for Lonely Planet / **38:** Jiayi Chen, via Wee Red Bar / **39:** Oskar Kirk Hansen, via Kafe Kweer / **40–41:** Kay Roxby/Alamy / **42:** Diana Laskaris and Sue Reddel; Teresa Lopes de Silva, via Pensão Amor / **42–43:** Maremagnum/ Getty Images / **44:** Jacek Sopotnicki/Getty Images / **44–45:** ESB Professional/Shutterstock / **46:** Teresa Lopes de Silva, via Pensão Amor / **47:** Nikolay Tsuguliev/Shutterstock / **48:** Carlos Neto/ Shutterstock / **49:** 1942 Productions / **50–51:** Rahil Ahmad / **51:** James Charles Abbott, via Dalston Superstore / **52:** Matt Munro for Lonely Planet / **53:** Hallie Primus, via Common Press / **54:** Café Comercial; Two Bad Tourists / **54–55:** Travelpix Ltd/Getty Images / **56:** Adrienne Pitts for Lonely Planet / **56–57:** Javitouh/ Shutterstock / **58:** Alex Segre/500px / **59:** Emilio Parra Doiztua for Lonely Planet / **60–61:** Blake Horn for Lonely Planet / **62:** Matt Munro for Lonely Planet / **63:** Gayly Planet / **64–65:** Kevin Faingnaert for Lonely Planet / **65:** Beatrice Bertone, via Antigone / **66:** Kevin Faingnaert for Lonely Planet / **67:** Camparino / **69:** Matt Munro for Lonely Planet / **70:** Johner Images/Getty Images ; The Beatnik Group / **70–71:** Mistervlad/Adobe Stock / **72:** Shutterstock / **72–73:** Erik Lernestål / **74:** Shutterstock / **75:** Shutterstock / **76:** Matt Munro for Lonely Planet / **77:** Anna Marie Felice / **78–79:** Matt Munro for Lonely Planet / **79:** Ġugar / **80:** Arcady/Shutterstock / **81:** Matthew Mirabelli for Lonely Planet / **82:** Michal Sarauer/Shutterstock; The Goldon Queers / **82–83:** annhfhung/Getty Images / **84:** That Feeling Co. / **84–85:** Troutnut/Shutterstock / **86:** Rob Daugherty/Design Pics/Getty Images / **87:** Cavan-Images/Shutterstock / **88–89:** Parker Everett/ Shutterstock / **90:** T Atkins/Grexsys, LLC/500px / **91:** Sam Slupski / **92–93:** Agave Photo Studio/Shutterstock / **93:** Oskar Bowin, via Tillery Street Plant Company / **94:** Kris Davidson for Lonely Planet / **95:** Kendrick Russell, via Proud Mary / **96:** girlseeingworld/Shutterstock; Leticia Souza Photography /

96–97: FilippoBacci/iStock / **98:** Bloomberg/Getty Images / **98–99:** Matt Munro for Lonely Planet / **100:** Osugi/Shutterstock / **101:** Noa Ratinsky/Shutterstock / **102:** Atmosphere1/Shutterstock / **103:** Cory Allen Hall / **104–105:** Jessica Vanterpool/FliSocial, via Sports Bra / **105:** Alanna Hale for Lonely Planet / **106:** Seagrape Apothecary / **107:** Meghan O'Dea for Lonely Planet / **108:** Shutterstock; Jasmine Conway / **108–109:** Ferran Traite/ Getty Images / **110:** Noah Sauve/Shutterstock / **110–111:** Marilyn Nieves/Getty Images / **112:** Tuned_In/Getty Images / **112–113:** Lindsay Lauckner Gundlock for Lonely Planet / **114:** Xavier Ascanio/Shutterstock / **115:** Paige Poprocky / **116–117:** Klaus Balzano/Shutterstock / **117:** Erin Cadigan/Shutterstock / **118:** Rachel Stolte / **119:** Robyn Bentley, via Diversity Thrift / **120–121:** Nat Thanapohn/Shutterstock / **122:** Dustin Tyler; Virtue Cider / **122–123:** Wirestock Creators/Shutterstock / **124:** Virtue Cider/ **124–125:** William Reagan/Getty Images / **126:** Sam Vargas Photography, via Dunes Resort / **127:** Samantha Denman, via Borrowed Time / **128–129:** Donna R. Theimer AIFD/Shutterstock / **130:** Michael Wels/Getty Images / **131:** megamouthmedia consulting / **132–133:** Yingna Cai/Shutterstock / **133:** Forbidden Vancouver Walking Tours, via The Really Gay History Tour/ **134:** LeonWang/Shutterstock/ **135:** Katt Talsma/500px / **136:** Aurelia St Clair; GOER/Shutterstock / **136–137:** Scott E Barbour/ Getty Images / **138:** THPStock/Getty Images / **138–139:** James Braund for Lonely Planet / **140:** James Braund for Lonely Planet / **141:** Sunflowerey/Shutterstock / **142:** Nelson Almeida/Getty Images / **143:** Clovis Casemiro / **144–145:** F de Jesus/Shutterstock / **145:** Everton Eifert/Shutterstock / **146:** Museum of Sexual Diversity/ **147:** Steve Outram/Getty Images / **148–149:** Cris Faga/ Shutterstock / **153:** Nick Fox/Shutterstock / **154–155:** Getty Images / **155:** Greg Ward/Shutterstock / **156–157:** Shutterstock / **158:** Daniel Freyr/Shutterstock / **159:** Matteo Colombo/ GettyImages / **161:** Lukasz Szwaj/Shutterstock / **162:** Cavan-Images/Shutterstock / **164–165:** Arpad Benedek/iStock / **166:** Noppasin/Shutterstock / **167:** Keitma/Shutterstock / **168–169:** Nan_Photography/Shutterstock / **171:** A. Aleksandravicius/ Shutterstock / **172–173:** Philip Thurston/Getty Images / **173:** Stephen B. Goodwin/Shutterstock / **174–175:** Shutterstock / **176:** Stephen Simpson/Getty Images / **177:** Victor Maschek/ Shutterstock / **179:** Stian Klo for Lonely Planet / **180–181:** Nataliya Hora/Shutterstock / **181:** Malcolm P Chapman/Getty Images / **182–183:** Artur Debat/Getty Images / **185:** Shutterstock / **186–187:** AsiaTravel/Shutterstock / **187:** Austin Bush for Lonely Planet / **188–189:** Shutterstock / **191:** Maxim Tupikov/ Shutterstock / **192–193:** Maximilian Müller/Getty Images / **193:** Shutterstock / **194–195:** Yvonne Navalaney/Shutterstock / **196:** Boris Stroujko/Shutterstock / **197:** Patrick Frilet/Shutterstock / **199:** Mara Brandl/imageBROKER/Shutterstock / **200:** NurPhoto/ Getty Images / **201:** Coke Bartrina for Lonely Planet / **202:** Oliver Foerstner/Shutterstock / **204:** Wolfgang Kaehler/Getty Images / **205:** Getty Images / **206:** Alyona Merriman/Shutterstock / **207:** Jordan Siemens/Getty Images / **217:** AJSTUDIO PHOTOGRAPHY/Shutterstock / **239:** GirlGoneAbroad

About the Author

Alicia Valenski is an American travel writer and editor living in the Netherlands. With a journalism degree from The Pennsylvania State University, she cut her teeth as a writer and editor at the *Charlotte Observer* before rising to the lofty heights of senior editor at *theSkimm*. Now, she's navigating life in Amsterdam with her partner, their dog, and a GPS that's forever confused by the city's endless bike paths. Alicia writes about the ups, downs, and sideways adventures of being a bisexual, neurodivergent expat, all with a generous dose of honesty, humor, and heart. When she's not exploring new places or sharing her stories, she's probably lost in a good book, perfecting her napping skills, or rewatching one of her comfort TV shows for the umpteenth time. You can find her on Substack at aliciavalenski.substack.com and on social media @aliciavalenski.

Project Editor Becca Hunt
Designers Emily Dubin, Wynne Au-Yeung
Editor Karyn Noble, Polly Thomas
Cartographer Wayne Murphy
Publishing Director Piers Pickard
Publisher Becca Hunt
Art Director Emily Dubin
Image Research Briana Ellis-Gibbs, Breanna Denney
Print Production Nigel Longuet

Written by Alicia Valenski

The LGBTQ+ Travel Guide
March 2025
Published by Lonely Planet Global Limited
CRN: 554153
ISBN: 9781837582716
www.lonelyplanet.com
© Lonely Planet 2025
10 9 8 7 6 5 4 3 2 1
Printed in China

STAY IN TOUCH
lonelyplanet.com/contact

Lonely Planet Office:
IRELAND
Digital Depot, Roe Lane (off Thomas St),
Digital Hub, Dublin 8, D08 TCV4, Ireland

Paper in this book is certified against the Forest Stewardship Council™ standards. FSC™ promotes environmentally responsible, socially beneficial and economically viable management of the world's forests.